INTERNAL SERVICE EXCELLENCE

A Manager's Guide to Building World Class
Internal Service Unit Performance

INTERNAL SERVICE EXCELLENCE

A Manager's Guide to Building World Class
Internal Service Unit Performance

Richard D. Hays

Summit Executive Press

Manufactured in the United States of America
Library of Congress Catalog Card Number: 96-11707
ISBN: 0-9651290-0-4

Author's photograph by permission, Olan Mills
Cover design: Pearl and Associates

Produced in association with Tabby House

Library of Congress Cataloging-in-Publication Data

Hays, Richard D.
    Internal service excellence : a manager's guide to building world class internal service unit performance / Richard D. Hays.
        p. cm.
    Includes bibliographical references and index
    ISBN 0-9651290-0-4
    1. In-house services (Business)--Quality control. 2. In-house services (Business)--Case studies. I. Title
HF5415.53.H39 1996
658.5'62--dc20   96-11707
                                                      CIP

Summit Executive Press
P.O. Box 5184
Sarasota, FL 34277
(941) 346-2227

Acknowledgments

The perspective, comments, and feedback of many business professionals and academics who are knowledgeable about internal service performance have contributed very significantly to this book. For their help I am most grateful.

Ian Arnof, President and CEO, *First Commerce Corporation*

David Bear, IS Manager, *ESSO InterAmerica, Inc.*

Lloyd Brubaker, Chief Operating Officer, *Wright, Lindsey & Jennings.*

Elaine Corum, Vice President, Training & Development, *Boatmen's National Bank of Arkansas, Inc.*

Gerry Leader, Professor, *Boston University School of Business*

Skip Kersey, Department Head, *Exxon Company, USA*

Robert McCammon, Manager of Human Resources *ESSO InterAmerica, Inc.*

Sherri Merl, Consultant, *Riverton Management Consulting*

Sue Nelkin, *University of New Orleans*

I am particularly indebted to Walter Eldredge (*Exxon Company, USA*), and James Granier (*First Commerce Corporation*) who each contributed amazingly high amounts of energy and practical insight toward the improvement of this book. Betsy Newberry added much to clarity and logic through her developmental editing.

However, there is one person who deserves special thanks, my respected professional colleague, my critic, my supporter, my parenting partner, and my wife, Dr. Joni Steinberg, who offered unending energy, technical contribution, and encouragement to bring this book to fruition.

Contents

Preface

As a business school professor during the 1970s, I began to see a series of important organizational problems that had a striking similarity. Later in the 1980s, as an executive charged with achieving turnarounds in several internal service units, the pattern became clear. Finally, as an organizational consultant, I have looked at this important set of issues in many client organizations in a variety of industries and settings and the picture has become ever more crisp. *Internal service units share a set of characteristics that make them the most underutilized source of new organizational performance breakthroughs in business today.*

Internal service units are big—representing almost 40 percent of employment in most firms. *They are important*—they are early and key contributors to a "chain of service" that ends with the final customer. *They are linked in concerns and issues*—sharing a common set of "critical success factors" and constraints. *They are a source of frustration*—most internal units are the targets of criticism for service which is often seen as ineffective and expensive. *They are low in historical performance attention*—most organizations have focused the bulk of productivity and effectiveness attention on the more public units. *They are ready for dramatic improvement*—a practical and proven method is available to produce strong performance turnarounds.

This book provides insights into the issues in internal service unit performance, as well as a practical and effective way to plan and execute internal service unit turnarounds. The first chapters explore the nature of the internal service crisis and the specific forces which create it. Subsequent chapters illustrate the analytic framework and action steps that are needed to engineer a turnaround in internal service performance. Appendices contain practical and proven survey instruments, interview outlines, and other "hands-on" material to help actually execute a renaissance in internal service unit performance.

Throughout the book, the exploration of these needs and remedies uses several parallel tools. An integrated text focuses on the primary issues at each stage of the exploration. In Parts II through VI, the text is augmented by a detailed case study of Mid-Americorp—an actual, but disguised company that typifies the issues facing most units that are trying to deal with these challenges. The case and the text in each chapter are examining the same conceptual territory, but are doing so from very different perspectives. Specific applications and examples are used throughout.

A total approach to managing an internal service unit turnaround is presented here. Remedy requires a steady and knowledgeable approach that exhibits both a solid commitment to change and skill in executing complex organizational change processes.

The intent of the book is to stimulate thoughtful insight into the problems and issues that face internal service organizations and to provide helpful action routes toward practical conversion of problems into performance. I hope that the ideas presented here will help you lead your organizations toward internal service excellence. I solicit your feedback on your personal experiences in applying this material, and on issues that you feel may help others in their quest to build world class internal service unit performance.

RICHARD D. HAYS
Sarasota, Florida
(941)346-2227 voice
(941)346-2440 fax
businesdoc@aol.com

PART I
THE INTERNAL SERVICE CRISIS
What is this problem of internal service?

Chapter 1

The Vital Role of Internal Service Units

In companies around the world, muted cries of pain and frustration swell into a chorus of discontent and exasperation. They are caused by internal service units that are unable to meet the service expectations and needs of the front line organizational units, despite strong efforts to provide good service. The front line, with ultimate customer contact or production responsibility, may have worked hard to understand customer needs and to meet them effectively and profitably. But success of this effort depends upon the quality, cost, and timeliness of the services and support provided by the "back office" or internal support units. The quality of support from service departments such as information systems, marketing, human resources, accounting/finance, facilities, maintenance, legal, purchasing, research and development, and headquarters can either bouy up or sink front line efforts to meet the needs of the ultimate customer.

For many of these troubled companies, efforts to enhance effectiveness and competitiveness have focused on the more visible line units. These efforts have usually achieved some gains, but have often fallen well short of the desired competitive impact. The reason: They are blunted by one vital missing element—*internal service excellence*. Any effort to improve overall organizational performance relies on the quality and dependability of services provided by members of the internal service units to others in the same company. This realization has allowed many organizations to shift focus and to build truly world class internal service performance, thus contributing dramatically to overall organizational results.

Internal Service Units:
Crucial Organizational Leverage Points

Internal service units are a large untapped resource for dramatic organizational performance improvement. They are:
- big,
- important,
- linked in concerns/issues,
- sources of strong frustration, and
- low in historical improvement attention.

Understanding their crucial role in the organization clarifies their potential competitive impact.

Internal Service Operations Are Big

As business organizations and marketplaces have grown in complexity, so have internal support organizations. Today, about 40 percent of employment and 45 percent of payroll in large corporations are generated by internal service units. Approximately 50 million U.S. workers are employed in these internal service units! For an individual organization, the massive costs represented by these units and the important services that they render are obvious, but often overlooked, arenas for significant organizational performance improvement.

Typical Internal Service Units:

Accounting	Administrative Services
Data Processing	Engineering
Facilities Management	Finance
Headquarters Office	Human Resources
Legal	Marketing
Medical	Public Relations
Purchasing	Research & Development

Internal Service Operations Are Important

The quality of internal services heavily shapes the process of building value for the ultimate customers. The value provided to that final customer is created through the contribution of a sequence of separate incremental actions, each a link in a "chain of value" that produces final customer need satisfaction. The last and most visible link in this chain, the ultimate customer contact, usually receives the most improvement attention. But the quality of that final product or service is the result of many, many prior steps of adding value to the developing product or service.

The initial tone and framework of the overall value-adding process, as well as much of the early value added itself, is established by the internal service units. The human resources department recruits and trains the individual employees that will work in the process. The marketing department researches the basic customer needs and determines the broad customer expectations. The research and development department performs the basic work that permits the emergence of a new product or service to fill the identified customer need. The accounting and finance departments provide the financial systems that allow product pricing and internal unit operation. By the time these and other internal service units have completed their work, a substantial portion of the final value has been added. Obviously, if the quality or effectiveness of this early and important contribution is flawed, a quality "ceiling" has been established for the final product or service.

The strong link between improved internal service and better service to external customers is becoming clear. External customer satisfaction depends upon teamwork and cooperation between internal service units and their internal customers. This concept has been referred to as the "service-profit chain," an idea that clarifies the importance of internal service.[1] Ultimate profit depends upon external customer loyalty, loyalty depends on customer satisfaction, customer satisfaction depends on the value created by employees, and employee satisfaction depends on quality internal support services. Internal service units are at an early and formative position in a chain of value-adding events that result in the ultimate product or service. Assuring that these early contributors in the chain of service are of the highest caliber is essential to high overall organizational performance.

Internal Service Operations Are Linked in Concerns/Issues

Various internal service units have widely differing primary technologies (information systems, marketing, finance, etc.). These more obvious differences often block awareness of the strong commonality of concerns and situations that link them together. Some of the issues shared by these internal service units are:

- Service unit performance success is measured by satisfaction of customer unit needs.

- They are in a monopoly situation (with the related advantages and problems).
- They have limited control of resources.
- They have shared noncustomer "stakeholders," those who have a high vested interest in internal service operations.

In many ways, the common agenda shared by internal service units is much stronger than their differences in technology. Recognizing this commonality can open the door to shared perspective and interaction on the issue of providing improved and cost-effective internal service.

Internal Service Units Are Sources of Strong Frustration

In all too many organizations the internal service units are under strong attack for poor service, high costs, or both. Line units complain about lumbering and insensitive service offered by uncaring and expensive people. Communications become clogged with complaints, accusations, and defenses and are relatively devoid of productive, service-related exchanges. On the other hand, the service unit sees itself as trying valiantly to produce solid, although unappreciated, services. Both sides become frustrated and angry. Attacks, rebuttals, positioning, and counterattack contribute nothing to the ultimate goals of the broader organization, but do take up a significant amount of time and energy. Everyone sees that this is nonproductive, but they feel trapped in roles that condemn them to conflict.

Internal Service Operations Have Had Relatively Low Amounts of Productivity Attention

Management theorist Peter Drucker has noted that, "the greatest challenge facing managers in the developed countries of the world is to raise the productivity of knowledge and service workers." The service sector, in general, and the internal service units in particular, have been relatively ignored in the quest for vastly improved productivity and quality. The services sector of the U.S. economy has grown to now constitute 80 percent of all employment—up from about 60 percent as recently as 1970. The productivity index for nonmanufacturing has grown only 5 percent in that period while productivity for manufacturing has grown 60 percent. This relatively low productivity improvement in services exists despite the fact that 85 percent of America's installed base of information technology is in

How Internal Service is Seen

In the summer of 1993, *Quality* magazine and Wm. Schiemenn & Associates (a Somerville, N.J., consulting company), launched an extensive survey of their readers regarding the perceived effectiveness of various internal service units. They received 841 responses from 39 different industries. When asked to rate overall service performance, respondents gave various internal departments these ratings:

INTERNAL SERVICE EFFECTIVENESS

DEPARTMENT	% FAVORABLE RESPONSES
Quality	48
Manufacturing/Production/Operations	42
Engineering	41
R & D	36
Finance/Accounting/Purchasing/Facilities	32
Marketing/Sales/Customer Service	31
MIS	28
Communication/Public Affairs/Legal	25
Human Resources	24

Obviously, internal service was not seen positively in this study. However, 59 percent of the departments rated had predicted that their customers would rate them favorably–almost twice the rate that actually did!

The study went on to examine the differences between those that scored particularly high in internal service ratings and those that scored low. Service leaders clearly had a much stronger propensity to have a clear service strategy, to use many measures of performance, and to approach service as an integrated, holistic process. This kind of organized and disciplined approach clearly pays strong dividends in improved internal service quality.

SOURCE: Mary Cronin Azzolini and John H. Lingle, "Internal Service Performance," *Quality*, 32,(Nov. 1993), pp. 38-40.

the service sector. Limited productivity gains in the service sector, coupled with the vast growth in absolute employment, has become a drag on productivity improvements for many individual businesses, and for the U.S. economy as a whole. Although more attention is now being given to improvement in the productivity of the services sector, little direct attention is going to the internal service units themselves.

Each of these characteristics illustrates the critical role internal service play in modern organizations. Unfortunately, in many cases they are not able to provide the excellence that is needed. When internal service is of low quality or is provided at high cost, the entire organization becomes impaired by the "pain" of poor service. This pain, just like physical human pain, may permit the organizational body to continue to function, but constrains overall performance to substandard levels.

Putting Chapter One Ideas to Work

Here are some specific questions to help promote thinking about how this material relates to your organization.

✓ Is *excessive cost* or *unresponsiveness* the major internal service complaint of customer units in your organization? How do these complaints manifest themselves in everyday work interactions? How much is being lost (time, organizational focus, or dollars) in arguments, concerns, and rebuttals about expensive or poor internal service within your organization?

✓ What percent of your organization's work force is in internal service units? What objective, evaluative data exists about the level of performance of the various internal service units? What is the general perception of the quality and efficiency of internal service units in your organization?

✓ Internal service units have a strong hand in shaping the early parts of the process of overall creation of final product or service value for the larger organization. In your own situation, in what specific ways is the contribution of internal service units at an early point in the chain of value creation impacting overall organizational performance and effectiveness?

Chapter 2

The Performance Crisis

Who Feels What About the Pain?

Organizations with internal service problems are made up of a variety of different individuals and groups, each of whom feels the pain of the internal service problem differently. No one is right or wrong, but each has a very different perspective on the problem caused by poor internal service.

The Pain from the CEO's Viewpoint

The CEO wants to identify and meet the needs of ultimate customers and, at the same time, keep support costs under control. As Peter Drucker points out, "Forty years ago, service and support costs accounted for no more than 10 percent or 15 percent of total costs. So long as they were so marginal, their low productivity did not matter. Now that they are more likely to take forty cents out of every dollar they can no longer be brushed aside."[1] And as organizations grow in complexity the need for excellent internal service expands.

For the CEO this means that poor and inadequate internal support systems can no longer be ignored. Overall organizational competitiveness hinges on fixing this problem. The cries of frustration and desperation from line division managers who feel that they are stymied in their efforts by poor or expensive internal support, find their way quickly to the CEO's office and must be handled. The CEO can also see that this conflict is absorbing vast amounts of internal organizational energy that could otherwise be channeled into productive efforts.

John Starr, president of Alcoa Separations Technology Inc., described the growth of the problem in his company this way:

> "Our organization, like so many in American industry, had become comfortable in our nice, protected world. We were competing in a growing business with a lot of opportunities. Not surprisingly, we had organized ourselves into functional departments and whenever costs would rise, we would send the sales and marketing teams out to raise prices. The world, however, started to change. Our competitors got a little better, our technical advantages (diminished), and *most importantly, as we grew, our internal groups lost contact with their customers and became more driven by their internal process than by what was really important to the customer.*"[2]

For the CEO, this problem continues to grow like a cancer in the organization until it escalates to crisis proportions, either through market performance pressures to grossly reduce costs, or through a rising chorus of internal complaints of poor service from line managers—either of which requires action! The CEO knows that something has to be done, but what?

The Pain from the Viewpoint of the Chief Financial Officer

For the CFO, these rising service costs are particularly frustrating. If overhead costs (mostly support units) are growing faster than revenues, a serious problem is developing. The real difficulty is in knowing what to do about it. Draconian across-the-board cuts are tempting, but typically only serve to further damage needed services and leave the core problem untouched. In the late 1980s, IBM Corporation began to see such impending problems, and took action to cut headquarters staff dramatically in a substantial restructuring. But overhead expenses kept rising. The problem was more fundamental than simply excess fat. For the CFO, the control of internal service cost growth in IBM or any organization can be vexing. Reversing the climb in these overhead costs is almost impossible without first getting to the real basis of the problem.

The CFO is strongly frustrated by the pattern of growth in internal costs. Individual internal service units naturally continue to press for bigger budgets in order to better render their services. However, the CFO understands that money doesn't cause quality; attitudes and good systems do. If the service of internal units is seen by line units as poor or unreliable, an insidious pattern develops. The line manager complains about poor internal service, but may get little or no change. The line manager then steps up the pressure for improvement, but finds how little direct control over the internal service units an outsider really has, and temporarily retreats in frustration. But the desired services are still needed. This frustration can prompt a quick (and quiet) move to create the same or similar services within the line organization so that direct control over quality and cost is possible. This is not an unreasonable strategy from the viewpoint of the individual manager, but it creates a growing concern for the CFO who now sees internal service production capabilities emerging within the line units themselves, duplicating services already offered by existing internal service units. Attempts to squash the line duplicates of internal services are met with great resistance and complaints from the line. The CFO knows that something has to be done, but what?

The Pain from the Viewpoint of the Internal Customer

For the head of a line unit who depends upon internal service units for support, the pain grows out of an exasperating lack of control. This manager knows that the line unit tries diligently to meet customer needs, but seems constantly blocked in its effort by the lack of proper internal support. The internal service units seem to have little feeling for the ultimate customer and the problems that the line manager faces in trying to meet their needs. Complaints about poor service are met with indifference and excuses about lack of resources, too many demands, etc. As the manager sees it, though, that is the job of the internal service divisions—to supply good service to the line divisions that actually bring in the money.

The line manager's initial approach to dealing with the problem is to gain preferential service attention by escalating the priority attached to service requests. However, other line divisions soon enter the competition and escalate their priority assertions too. Everyone quickly falls back into the same frustrating situation.

In addition, the costs of internal services seem to be far beyond what is necessary. The line manager knows of similar services that are available outside the company which can be purchased for much less than the company is now paying for these internal services.

As frustration grows over the lack of control of the deteriorating situation, the line manager may conclude that the best option is to set up a source of supply for this service that is totally internal to the line operation—that way both service quality and costs can be controlled directly. But this move will be resisted by the internal service units and by top management. The heads of the internal customer divisions know that something must be done—but what?

The Pain from the Viewpoint of the Internal Service Unit

The person responsible for the internal service unit may be in the most pain of all. This manager is trying desperately to render the best service possible at a reasonable cost. Workers in the internal service unit are giving strong efforts to accomplish this, but are constrained on several sides by forces that limit their ability to act. The manager's internal customers have an ever-increasing barrage of demands for special services that swamp well-established procedures. They also show little understanding for the need for professionalism and the problems and limitations of providing good internal service. The users seem to constantly surprise the service unit with needs that they say have not been met.

The internal service unit manager is trapped in a degenerating cycle of demands, criticism, and artificially trumpeted priorities followed by even stronger internal service efforts to supply more and better service. The only result seems to be an escalation in the complaints. To make matters worse, pressure is mounting from the CEO to be more responsive to the line managers. The CFO, too, is pressuring the internal service unit to contain what he calls "run-away costs." The situation seems even more bleak when several line managers are discovered clandestinely constructing their own internal service units. These actions exacerbate the situation by driving up unit costs within the internal service unit due to decreasing economies of scale. The head of the internal service unit knows that something must be done— but what?

The Pain from the Viewpoint of the Ultimate Customer

When the company is having internal service problems, the ultimate customer—the one who buys the company's end product or service— feels the pain too. The external customer receives lower value at higher cost because of internal service problems. How often has each of us heard a salesperson, when confronted by a lack of internal support from their own operation, say, "I would love to help you, but our computers are down again?" That's a thinly veiled version of: "Those idiots in the back office can't ever seem to keep them running." Or, have we heard, "Our policies just won't let me do that (even though I think that I should)?" The salesperson is not trying to be disloyal to the company, but is frustrated by a lack of internal support—a frustration that spills visibly into interactions with the ultimate customer. The customer sees these symptoms as a lack of professionalism and feels decreased satisfaction of needs. It won't be long before the customer moves to another company that may be able to do better.

The ultimate customer knows that something should be done—but could care less about some remote "internal problem." The customer has options and will use them!

The Joy from the Viewpoint of the Corporate Raider

As the internal service problem worsens, the pain felt inside the company is matched by the joy felt by the raider. The corporate raider is looking for pools of waste and inefficiency within a target organization that could be eliminated or turned around in a purchase or merger. A company becomes a particularly tempting morsel for takeover if an internal service problem has gone unaddressed for some time. A multiplicity of duplicated services and the growing conflict within absorbs vast amounts of internal energy that otherwise could be profitably applied to the ultimate customer. Sir Gordon White, the chairman of Hanson Industries Limited (known for its acquisitions), has observed that "corporate headquarters are another treasure trove waiting to be discovered." He sees the potential clearly. The corporate raider knows that something must be done—and may know just what!

The Crisis Deepens

Each of the players in the developing situation has a perspective derived from his or her own needs and interactions. But there are four commonly found organizational forces that act as basic causal agents to help create this negative state of affairs. Some or all of these forces are visibly present and active in seriously troubled internal service units. They are inherent in the internal service situation and act in ways that create, and then sustain, a *conflict-dominated climate*. Unless aggressively countered, they will steadily propel the organization into more negative interactions where those involved become trapped in behaviors and roles that exacerbate the conflict. These basic causal forces are:

1. *The apparent monopoly.* Internal service units are inherently susceptible to a comforting, but false assumption that they are in possession of a monopoly for their particular service. Few internal service units would overtly label themselves as being in a monopoly position as a service provider, but the reality is that the assumption of monopoly does exist in many cases and does define behavior. Most internal service units have functioned for years as the sole provider of their particular service for their internal customer units, thereby confirming this assumption even further. If not confronted, this assumption creates strong friction between service user and service supplier.

2. *Internally driven culture.* A second powerful force that shapes the behavior and function of an internal service unit is its culture. Every unit has a culture which influences how it sees itself, how it does its work, and how it relates to others outside the unit. Each culture is shaped by a few dominant values. In many internal service units the value of *technical excellence* dominates the culture. This is a natural and comfortable value. After all, technical excellence and competence probably attracted most employees of the unit to their profession. But this value reinforces an internal focus of attention and effort, rather than a focus on the needs of the customer units. Some insightful internal service units have carefully analyzed the overall organizational impact of having technical excellence as a central value and have concluded that they cannot achieve their service goals with this culture in place. They have determined that this technical ethic must be displaced from its sole central position and must be replaced by a value of *service to customers*.

3. *Poorly defined expectations/poorly measured results.* Many relationships between internal service units and their customer units are plagued by vague definitions of service expectations and poor or nonexistent measurement systems for service performance. Most customer units have only vague and imprecise service expectations. They have had

Symptoms of Serious Internal Service Problems

How much of an internal service problem does your organization have? Think of the internal service units (ISUs) within your company—any internal department whose primary function is to provide service to other departments. They could be groups such as Information Systems, Human Resources, Marketing, Engineering, Accounting, etc. Pick the one ISU that you want to examine and circle one response to each of the six questions below that best describes it.

SYMPTOM	*DESCRIBES OUR SITUATION*				
1. A high state of conflict and disagreement between this unit and customer units is a continuing and dominant feature of their ongoing relationship	not at all				exactly
	1	2	3	4	5
2. Customer units complain loudly and insistently about poor internal service or the high cost of service from this unit	not at all				exactly
	1	2	3	4	5
3. Customer units attempt to build their own internal duplicates of this unit's service in order to gain better control	not at all				exactly
	1	2	3	4	5
4. Senior corporate executives are very frustrated with seemingly uncontrolled costs in the ISU and with the continuing need to "referee" conflicts between the ISU and its customer units	not at all				exactly
	1	2	3	4	5
5. Considerable executive and managerial time, energy, and effort is being expended in dealing with interdepartmental conflict issues or in "positioning" for possible future conflicts	not at all				exactly
	1	2	3	4	5
6. The conflicts over internal service or high costs are beginning to have an impact on the interface with our ultimate customers	not at all				exactly
	1	2	3	4	5

little incentive to explore and precisely define what they really need from the internal service unit. The result, then, is usually "unacceptable." Service providers must assertively work with their customer units to define and clearly articulate their expectations and the standards of service they receive. Without the *prior* specification of service expectations and standards, the service unit is destined to become mired in a role of "defender" of the service that has already been rendered and judged inadequate—hardly a position that will prompt improved service or lower costs.

4. *Inefficient service offering.* An internal service unit that strives to do well may be tempted to offer to do anything for anyone in the name of good service. As a result, many service units find themselves caught in a complexity trap. The unit has, over time, created a set of customized and unique service offerings for many small groups of internal customers that is complex, cumbersome, and expensive. Two important side effects of this are *higher costs* and *lower quality.* For the internal service unit, the goal of achieving consistently excellent service at reasonable cost is made impossible by its attempts to offer an ill-defined and broad set of services. The intent may be admirable, but the result is unreliable and expensive service.

Each of these forces (explored more fully in Chapter Five) occurs naturally in most internal service situations. Unless they are directly countered, the stage is set for the emergence of even more negative forces (Chapter Six) and an internal service crisis that absorbs massive amounts of organizational energy and effectiveness.

Putting Chapter Two Ideas to Work

Here are some specific questions to help promote thinking about how this material relates to your organization.

✓ In your own situation, who are the main players that have an important stake in the performance of the internal service unit? How is your current internal service situation seen by each of them? What does each of them want to see happen in terms of ultimate results?

✓ On a scale of 1 to 10 (1 = very low, 10 = very high), how strongly do people in your organization feel about the need to fundamentally change the internal service situation? (How much "pain" is being felt about the current situation?)

✓ Beliefs about the causes and desirable corrective actions for internal service problems can vary immensely as seen in this chapter. In your organization what are the main differences in belief about the *causation* of difficulties? What are the main differences in belief about the nature or responsibility for *correction* of the problems? How are these differences in basic theories causing conflict and inefficiency?

✓ In what ways do you see a downward spiral of relationship quality between internal service units and their customer units? What factors are contributing most strongly to this deterioration?

Chapter 3

The Manager's Action Alternatives

Three specific and practical action alternatives are available to address the internal service problem—each with its own payoffs and costs.

Option One: Status Quo

The most obvious and, unfortunately, the most commonly used option is to maintain the status quo—to let things remain as they are. This option has low payoffs, but significant costs. For the CEO (usually the decision maker here), the press of other matters and the hope that the conflict will resolve itself delays any intervention. Often, some minor actions will temporarily ease the pain and quell the fighting. Pressure on the service unit to minimize complaints from their customers can bring some relief.

But such short-term solutions fail to confront and deal with the real underlying situation. These require significant expenditure of resources without real effect. For example, if the beleaguered head of an information systems department (the service provider) sees *the problem* as one of inadequate computer capacity, he might press for the costly solution of adding more computing power. This is a "quick fix," but it only masks the real problem of service delivery. Only *after* these underlying service problems are identified and dealt with can other issues such as the determination of proper computing capacity be addressed objectively. This option may seem appealing on the surface, but electing it only delays selecting one of the other options later.

Option Two: Outsourcing the Service

Many companies have become so tired of the internal service bickering and of repeated futile attempts at solution, that they have elected to spin off the work of some of their internal service units through "outsourcing." While finding outside suppliers for these services may be the right move for some organizations, it's often a decision that's made through frustration rather than through objective business analysis. Outsourcing does involve risk and many organizations have found that the loss of control and flexibility is greater than they had thought.

Before outsourcing an internal operation, a company should compare a well-functioning internal service unit to the best outside alternatives. But no well-functioning unit may be available for comparison purposes. In most cases, an outside supplier is *better* than a poorly functioning internal unit, but is *inferior* to a well-functioning internal unit. The significant loss of control and flexibility that comes with outsourcing is often enough to tip the decisional scales toward keeping many services internal, but only if the internal unit shows the potential to deliver excellent and cost-sensitive services. For many then, this second option resolves into how to produce a well-functioning internal service unit, either for retention or for a more rational comparison in evaluating outsourcing options.

Option Three: Creating an Internal Service Renaissance

During the fifteenth and sixteenth centuries, Europe was experiencing a cultural rebirth. Old ideas and standards were being challenged and replaced by newer ones that promoted more open, scientific thinking and creativity. The Renaissance produced a new framework for enormous progress.

In a very similar manner, the option to produce a renaissance in internal service operations exists with the same kind of dramatic payoffs in productivity and contribution. The change requires a similar fundamental rethinking of assumptions and approaches. Such a renaissance is focused on making the changes needed to bring actual internal service unit performance into the arena of excellence. It is certainly the most challenging and, if executed properly, the most effective option, but it is viable only if approached with resolution, knowledge, and skill.

A successful renaissance requires a firm resolution to proceed with a complete turnaround of the internal service unit rather than a

Pearl Harbor and Internal Service

The "backstage" nature of internal service unit performance can often have very public and significant results. One dramatic example of the consequences of internal service problems can be seen in the United States' inability to properly anticipate the December, 1941, attack on Pearl Harbor. Although many factors contributed to this failure, the poor functioning of the internal service units of the U.S. military played a large role.

In the years preceding Pearl Harbor, sophisticated code-breaking and intelligence activities were just beginning to develop in the U.S. military. Unfortunately, the evolution of a structure for the internal service organizations which focused on these activities was determined largely by turf wars and personal ambition, rather than by a quest for effective organizational support for line military units.

Effective intelligence efforts require excellence in the processes of gathering information (including code-breaking), analyzing it, and communicating results. The U.S. Navy had set up the Office of Naval Intelligence (ONI) whose original charge was to manage all intelligence matters. But over the years, a power struggle for the control of intelligence information resulted in many important pieces of the process being delegated to the Office of Naval Communications (ONC). By 1941, competition between these two internal support units had resulted in a severe separation of control of intelligence resources. ONI was responsible for code-breaking of the primary Japanese operational code, but *not for analysis*. ONC was responsible for overall political assessment, interpretation, and the fleet and diplomatic codes. ONC's responsibilities were more encompassing despite their substantially lower code breaking competence. Each organization only had a piece of the intelligence puzzle and, thus was not able to fully interpret its own information or to provide the whole perspective so desperately needed by the President and U.S. commanders.

During the first few days of December, 1941, important pieces of the intelligence picture were beginning to emerge in several separate segments of the Navy, but no one person or office had all of the data and perspective needed at the crucial time. The segmentation of responsibilities and the ambiguity of roles in these two Navy internal service units had virtually assured that the Japanese attack would be a surprise. The horrific results of this internal service failure are now an infamous part of American history. Internal service units in any type of organization can become so poorly structured or positioned as to render the production of quality service almost impossible! The results for the organization can be disastrous.

SOURCE: Rear Admiral Edwin T. Layton, *And I Was There: Pearl Harbor and Midway–Breaking the Secrets*, (New York: Quill, 1985).

piecemeal approach. It requires knowledge and a comprehensive plan that will make the change effective. Finally, it requires skill in executing a complex internal service unit change. A proven structure for achieving such a turnaround is covered in the following chapters. Only through this option can the full competitive power of internal service organizations be unleashed for the organization.

The Payoffs for Excellence in Internal Service

A successful renaissance in internal service performance can result in significant payoffs for the organization.

- *It can dramatically increase internal service productivity.* The internal service unit that has experienced a successful and service-oriented turnaround finds that time and energy formerly devoted to preparing for and dealing with conflict with users is now available for actual service enhancement. Interaction with users is now "problem-solving" in nature rather than conflictual. And, the effort spent in the initial stages of turnaround in analyzing and understanding their own business invariably pays strong dividends in more efficient and effective operation. Morale in the internal service unit improves as it moves out of the organizational doghouse and becomes a valued corporate contributor. Productivity gains of 20 percent to 60 percent are cited by many executives in successful turnarounds. Multiplied by the 40 percent internal service stake in employment, this translates into a striking gain in overall organizational productivity.

- *A renaissance can elevate overall quality ceilings.* Because internal service units are strong early contributors in the value-adding process, dramatic improvement in their performance removes artificial ceilings on the final quality of the product or service delivered to the external customer. Front-line organizations are released to produce their own quality limits unimpeded by internal service limitations. Internal service turnarounds place new and positive quality pressures on front-line units. They are forced to look within themselves for potential improvement rather than blaming others for overall performance limitations. Line unit efforts are truly empowered through the provision of quality internal services.

- *A renaissance can develop new sources of competitive advantage.* Some companies have developed such strong and effective internal service competencies that they now constitute a prime source of competitive advantage. American Airlines has long used its computing capability and unique software as a fundamental competitive advantage. Federal Express Corporation has dominated its market through excellence in internal systems. Otis Elevator Company and United Services Automobile Association both use their highly sophisticated and effective imaging systems as a source of strategic leverage. The consumer research function within the Procter & Gamble Company has accounted for much of the company's competitive prowess over the years. In each of these cases, an internal service unit has developed so strongly that it has become a source of primary competitive advantage for the entire corporation.

Internal service units can move from the doldrums of organizational problems to become a real source of competitive energy and drive. One of the most exciting and positive options available to internal service units today is to accept the challenge to deliver excellent customer service.

Putting Chapter Three Ideas to Work

Here are some specific questions to help promote thinking about how this material relates to your organization.

✓ In your organization, how satisfied are the various key players with the "status quo" option?

  • Is there a strong felt need to change?

  • Have specific proposals for change been offered? What are they? Offered by whom?

✓ How actively has "outsourcing" been discussed as a solution to your internal service problems?

✓ What pressures exist in your organization to settle for a relatively minor tuning of the current situation rather than a major change effort? If some early progress (lessening of the "pain") is made as a result of initial change efforts, will the organizational motivation to continue through the entire change process to a full and permanent solution be blunted?

PART II
THE FORCES AT WORK
What causes this problem?

Introduction

Creating a renaissance in internal service unit performance begins with a solid understanding of the negative forces that are inherent in internal service situations. This part of the book begins with a case study of a real company—which we are calling "Mid-Americorp"— that is experiencing serious internal service problems—the issues, problems, and solutions are real, only the names are changed. This case study illustrates the situation facing the information systems unit of a bank, but the details we discuss could just as easily be about the technical support department of a refinery, the marketing department of a manufacturing company, or the human resources department of a sales organization. These, and all other internal service units, face a common set of forces that are discussed here. The first part of the case, Mid-Americorp—The Performance Problem, focuses on the initial service difficulties faced by the information systems division. The other two chapters in Part II examine the same set of issues from a more encompassing and analytical perspective. This format of two parallel views is continued in subsequent parts of the book.

CASE: Mid-Americorp — The Performance Problem

In the spring of 1993, several states had enacted legislation that allowed banks to acquire other banks across state boundaries. Mid-Americorp, a large bank holding company located in the Midwest, used this opportunity to acquire six banks in contiguous states and almost double the holding company assets to over $10 billion. But CEO Jonathan Greyson had concerns. Much of the economic benefit from bank acquisition is derived from the savings in merging "back office" operations, particularly the computer systems and operations functions. In fact, initial analysis indicated that the savings from successful integration of these functions in the newly expanded company could result in an annual savings of over $7 million—a very significant plum for earnings if it could be obtained.

But Mid-Americorp's Information Systems (IS) Division was suffering from problems that posed a serious threat to realization of that savings potential. The division was poorly regarded within the company. Greyson received complaints continually about the division's undependable service and its apparent disregard for costs. He felt that the key to obtaining the savings lay in executing a significant and prompt turnaround in the IS Division. He faced a real challenge and began to survey the situation.

The Organization of Mid-Americorp

With its acquisitions, Mid-Americorp now owned banks in four Midwestern states through thirteen local bank operating companies. The thirteen local operations each had their own president and a branch network that utilized centralized support services from Mid-Americorp headquarters in Indianapolis. One of the most crucial support services was the IS Division. It encompassed both the operations department, which handled the actual processing of the 2.2 million checks that Mid-Americorp deals with each day, and the data processing department, which was the operator and custodian of the computer hardware and software of the company. The head of the IS Division, David Rawls, was highly respected for his solid technical computer knowledge. He reported directly to Greyson.

Feedback on the IS Division

The presidents of the six newly acquired banks had not yet formed any opinions about IS services. But the heads of the seven original Mid-Americorp banks submitted complaints almost daily to Greyson about the service that the IS Division was rendering, and the way the division dealt with the various bank units. This dissatisfaction had existed for some time, but dramatically intensified in the last year.

As he looked into the problem, Greyson found that until about a year ago, each bank president had given substantial feedback to the IS Division by talking directly to Rawls. They had service expectations that the IS Division did not recognize as valid. As criticism increased, Rawls became more remote and hostile, and he was seen as increasingly unresponsive. The presidents had shifted the focus of their complaints directly to Greyson in hope of gaining improvement in IS performance.

Specifically, the presidents saw the IS Division as more concerned about its own hardware and technology than about the needs and problems of the individual bank units it served. IS personnel seemed indifferent or even openly hostile when approached about new issues or problems. Pressure by the banks for IS to solve what they saw as serious service shortfalls often resulted in responses like: "We know what services you need and you are getting them." Frustration and hostility ran high within the banking units and within IS.

Greyson met with Mark Alexander, his chief financial officer, to gain more insight into the problem and found that Alexander also was very concerned. In each of the last three annual budget cycles, Alexander had been confronted with what amounted to an ultimatum from Rawls demanding new and very expensive major computer equipment for the IS Division. The justification for the new equipment request was in "computereze" that no one outside the IS Division could understand. But Rawls made it clear that unless the demanded equipment was purchased, the IS Division would have to significantly cut its services to all parts of the company. Alexander was disturbed that these budget standoffs had been resolved more through power and blustering than by the reasoned analysis that he saw as essential to a sound budgeting process.

In addition, Alexander noticed a lack of internal cost sensitivity and value-consciousness within the IS Division which was resulting in a steady increase in IS costs. One of his biggest concerns was with the duplication of services that he saw emerging. As the individual banks became more and more frustrated with the service and treatment they received from the IS Division, they began to create their own internal services to sidestep the frustration of dealing with IS. The most troublesome example was in the area of personal computers and networks. The IS Division was in charge of PCs, PC training, and networks throughout the company. But some of the presidents were attempting to build their own private systems that they felt better met their needs. Unfortunately, these individual systems were often incompatible with other company systems, and were installed in inefficient and expensive ways. In some cases, they duplicated capabilities already in the central systems or caused major drains on central computer capacity. Alexander felt that overall company costs were being seriously impacted by the problems of the IS Division.

The IS Division Perspective

As Greyson talked to Rawls about the situation, another perspective emerged. When Rawls had been hired six years ago, the IS Division was in the technological stone age. Rawls had been recruited to bring Mid-Americorp up-to-date in computing and operations technology and had done so with excellence. He had assembled a cadre of experienced technical people reporting to him, and they had completely renovated the way Mid-Americorp handled its information processing and operations tasks. In fact, the IS Department exhibited such strong technical competence that a major computer vendor had chosen the Mid-Americorp shop as a demonstration site for potential computer customers.

Many of the bank presidents, however, were unimpressed by this technical prowess. They were unsophisticated regarding computers and bank operations such as check and payments processing, and often made demands for services that were not compatible with IS capabilities or practicalities. Although Rawls did not have specific service standards or measures, it was clear to him that excellent service was being rendered to the banks—they just didn't have the sophistication to appreciate it. When something did go wrong, the presidents immediately seemed to "go into orbit" and exhibited no patience or understanding of systems problems and complications. Rawls felt that they had little appreciation for the technical excellence they were getting, or the hard work that the IS staff expended on their behalf. Any thanks for a job well done had to come from within the IS group itself.

Rawls found himself spending at least half of his time arguing with bank units about the service that they were getting from IS. What the presidents saw as service shortcomings were, upon investigation, often problems that the banks themselves were creating. But the IS Division got saddled with the blame for the problem anyway. To Rawls, it seemed the presidents were just looking for things to complain about and blamed many of their own performance shortfalls on IS service. He felt that only the firm stand that he had taken with them in these kinds of situations had saved the company from needless and expensive investigation of nonexistent problems and unfounded complaints. Rawls was getting very frustrated. He told Greyson that he had come to Mid-Americorp "to build a great IS Division, not to hand-hold people who didn't understand high standards or solid technology."

The CEO's Problem

Jonathan Greyson had a real problem and he knew it. The IS Division seemed to feel little need to improve performance— performance that was getting worse day-by-day. Rawls was upset about the treatment that the IS Division was getting and by what he saw as a lack of top management support. The individual bank presidents were getting more agitated about the poor IS service that was negatively impacting their operations, and they were now beginning to act together to press for change. The worries about increasing IS costs and waste were also growing. And, finally, the prospect of the $7 million in annual consolidation savings loomed large, but would evaporate without a successful turnaround in the situation.

Greyson knew that something had to be done, but what?

Putting Chapter Four Ideas to Work

Here are some specific questions to help promote thinking about how this material relates to your organization.

- ✓ In what ways is the discontent and concern about internal service seen in Mid-Americorp similar to or different from that which is expressed in your organization?

- ✓ Senior managers in Mid-Americorp seem to see the situation somewhat differently than the head of the internal service division. What forces are at work to cause this difference in perception? Which of these same forces also are active within your own organization? What is the impact of these differences in your organization?

- ✓ How does the "pain" of poor internal service reach the CEO of your organization? What is the CEO's reaction? What would the CEO really like to see happen?

Chapter 5

The Underlying Causal Forces

The Debilitating Forces

In the case of Mid-Americorp, and other internal service situations, several forces are working simultaneously to undermine relationships and service between the service unit and its customers. Causal forces, inherent in the basic service situation, cause the problem. Emergent forces arise later as the situation begins to deteriorate, adding to the problem. These sets of forces are the focus of Chapters Five and Six and are listed below.

Debilitating Forces in Internal Service

Causal forces (inherent in the internal service situation)
- The apparent monopoly
- Internally driven culture
- Poorly defined expectations/poorly measured results
- Inefficient service offering

Emergent forces (become active as the situation deteriorates)
- Deteriorating trust
- Defensive internal climate

Causal Forces

Causal forces are embedded in the internal service situation and foster a deterioration in the relationship between service supplier and internal customer. Unless these primary forces are understood and dealt with effectively, real progress toward dramatically improved internal service performance is blocked. Let's look at these forces.

The Apparent Monopoly

It's easy for an internal service unit to believe they hold a monopoly position as a supplier of specific services. The position has been secure in the past and it's difficult to see how any outsider could supply the needed insights and knowledge to act as a replacement. But a quick look at the current state of outsourcing shakes this belief.

Outsourcing is an action by a company to replace internally supplied services with those supplied by an independent outside firm — a move that has become common practice in U.S. business. The outsourcing market for information systems alone is over $20 billion and is projected to grow dramatically. Continental Bank, for example, sold its entire information technology division — formerly considered a prime source of competitive advantage. Eastman Kodak moved most of its information processing function to outside suppliers, and Xerox completed a $3 billion deal to have Electronic Data Systems run its worldwide computer systems.

Such strategic moves involving thousands of employees in large companies are highly publicized. But smaller companies, too, are outsourcing services with an overall impact that is at least as large. Outsourcing is a strong trend as businesses attempt to dramatically improve competitiveness by ridding themselves of poorly performing or costly internal service units.

Despite the trend toward outsourcing, many internal service units still operate as though they hold an unshakable monopoly position. Their historical security and the comfort that this illusion creates for some internal service units act to reinforce this belief.

The internal service unit's belief in the invincibility of its monopoly position may be strong, but it usually remains as an unspoken part of the culture that has far-reaching effects. It permeates all relationships of the service unit and heavily influences the way individuals within the unit see themselves, their jobs, and, most importantly, their role relative to their customer units.

Apparent monopoly situations have frequently become death spirals for entire companies. Here's a common scenario:

Stage 1   Establishment of a strong internal belief in the invincibility of a monopoly position.

Stage 2   Deterioration in attention to real customer needs and in the passion to fulfill those needs.

Stage 3   Entry of a new, competitive means to satisfy customer needs or undetected movement in the nature of the need.

Stage 4   Erosion of competitive position due to weak insight into customer needs and low ability to meet needs.

Unfortunately, the companies that are displaced by this scenario rarely see the forces gathering until it is much too late. This same cycle applies just as directly to internal service units. Troubled internal service units are often found at the second stage in this process — deterioration in attention to real customer needs.

The marketing department in a large hospital holding company provides a solid example of this problem. The department has won national awards and professional acclaim for its highly sophisticated advertising program. Unfortunately, the CEOs of the individual hospitals in the chain have not been as impressed. They did not see support of their local objectives in the marketing department actions, and approached the marketing department with their concerns. The marketing department was shocked and affronted by what they saw as criticisms by "nonprofessionals." The department told the CEOs that they were getting *very* sophisticated service (and, only thinly veiled was the underlying message of "but, you probably aren't sophisticated enough to appreciate it!"). The high price tag of the programs only added to the conflict (the CEOs were billed through for the cost). As their complaints were rebuffed, the CEOs began to see the marketing department as incapable of delivering the kind of service they needed and as creating a needless cost for the corporation. Complaints and rebuttal fed the mounting frustration until the CEOs launched a serious attempt to totally disband the marketing department and contract marketing services to outsiders. Only then did the marketing department begin to challenge their own internal assumptions about their seemingly unique position as service supplier.

The threat of losing its monopolistic position can force the internal service unit to rethink the way it does business. Many companies have experimented with the creation of internal market economies in which the service units assume the direct responsibility to produce and market their own services profitably. They are free to market both inside and outside the company, and their former "captive" internal clients are free to purchase the internal services, or to go out-

Organization Theory and the Internal Service Unit

James D. Thompson was the first organizational theorist to suggest that organizations seek to insulate their "technical core" (the production process in manufacturing firms or the customer contact elements in service firms) by building "buffer elements" (other departments or divisions) to insulate them from "environmental contingencies." The world simply provides too many distracting demands and the core elements of a business need to keep their attention focused on the primary task. Therefore, an organization tends to build various internal units to handle specific key inputs that are needed by the core units. Thus, the emergence of the "internal service unit."

More recently, Larry Hirschhorn has observed that it is quite natural for organizations to build boundaries around these internal organizational units as a way of coping with the anxiety and tension that builds up at the interface between them. Unfortunately, a related natural response is for the members of the units to "retreat from these boundaries" to provide additional personal comfort and put distance between them and these anxieties. Personal comfort can be increased even more as members within the internal service unit strengthen the bonding and sense of alliance that they feel toward each other (and, perhaps, even some shared sense of antipathy toward "outsiders" in other units).

When the members of the internal service unit retreat from the boundaries they actually begin a process of distancing themselves from the needs of their "customers." Intimacy with these needs can only be maintainied if these forces are aggressively countered through the creation of specific "boundary-spanners," individuals and groups whose mission is to foster the flow of needed information and perspective across the organizational boundaries–particularly the boundary with the customer units.

SOURCES: James D. Thompson, *Organizations in Action: Social Science Bases of Administrative Theory,*(New York: McGraw-Hill, 1967), and Larry Hirschhorn, *The Workplace Within: Psychodynamics of Organizational Life*, (Cambridge: MIT Press, 1988).

side. These experiments have produced a full range of successes and failures, but have always forced a quick and substantial revision of internal service cultures. Ford Motor Company, MCI Telecommunications, Alcoa, Dow Corning Corp., Control Data Corporation, and Esso Canada have all attempted to create versions of internal market economies. Jim Rinehart, former CEO at Clark Equipment Co., described how Clark was able to establish an internal market for services and shrink the 500-person corporate office to a 75-person operation:

"Our first step was to identify possible businesses encompassed within the corporate office. The list included a law firm, an accounting firm, a data processing/telecommunications company, a trucking company, and a printing and graphics company. These units were given two years to accomplish two goals: to have 50 percent of their business outside Clark and to earn their cost of capital.

"After one year, Clark's operating companies were no longer required to use the internal services. If a unit met the two criteria, it had three choices: 1) to become a Clark operating company; 2) to undertake an employee buyout; or 3) to find itself a new owner. If a unit failed to meet the criteria, option number one was not available. The result was three buyouts, one sale, and one new Clark operating company...over the last ten years (Clark Equipment has gone) from the brink of bankruptcy to the point of world cost and quality competitiveness."[1]

The Clark tactic was severe, driven by corporate survival threats. Clearly, several internal service units found the needed change more than they could manage.

As Alcoa moved toward a freer internal services market, they chose to insulate their R&D unit a bit more than in the Clark case. They were able to convert an unresponsive and expensive unit into one with both high customer responsiveness and with 35 percent of budget being funded from external sources:

"R&D always complained that the marketing groups (of Alcoa) were too short-term oriented and did not understand the complexities of longer-term development. The business units complained that R&D never could finish anything, was prohibitively expensive, and was always off working on some harebrained idea rather than getting the things done that would yield revenue sometime in this century.

"After we put the (internal market structure) in place, R&D did some serious reflection. They realized that their internal customers had only a limited budget for longer-term work. Given this understanding, they decided to reorient themselves to better satisfy their customers' requests by focusing on some of the hot projects emerging from the business units. Knowing that this would not satisfy their own internal desires for more creative and challenging projects, they decided to see if they (could obtain) funding from various outside groups and agencies that might value their expertise."[2]

Moving to a full internal market economy for services may not be appropriate for many organizations. But any opening of internal markets pushes service units to develop new skills to succeed outside the protective frame of a monopolistic situation. The most important of these required new skills is the ability to market their services. In traditional systems the internal service unit may not even be required to be diplomatic, much less to really care about and understand the basic needs of their customer units. Creating this marketing mentality within the internal service unit is an important step in challenging the premise of an apparent monopoly.

Internally Driven Culture

Every organizational unit has its own culture, made up of shared values and informal rules. This culture helps shape how the organization sees itself and its task, and how it gets its work done. It also provides group members with an unwritten guide on what the organization is, how it relates to others in the company, how it does its work, and its central driving values. Motorola and Xerox, for example, are renown for having cultures that are based on quality processes. Apple Computer is known for a culture that fosters innovation, and Procter & Gamble for its cultural focus on superior understanding of customer needs. The culture might be highly focused, as is often the case in older, more established units or those which have had a firm and directed leadership. These stronger and clearer cultures have considerable influence over the behavior of individuals. The culture in other units might be considerably weaker and more diffuse, but it still shapes behavior and organizational performance. Understanding the central elements of the culture of an organization is vital to dealing effectively with internal service issues.

Each culture is driven by one or more main themes. Some insight into these themes might be gained by looking at formal statements of mission and objectives (but they often vary considerably from the real drivers of the culture). A theme that must be central to an excellent internal service organization is an obsession with the needs of customer units. But another theme is prominent in most troubled internal service organizations—technical excellence.

Internal service units commonly are comprised of individuals who have strong training in and affiliation with a profession, such as law, marketing, human resources, computer systems, or accounting. They have a strong link to their professional group and feel a need to increase their technical expertise—a worthy goal. Within each service unit, individuals of like orientation and training are grouped together and interact frequently, thus reinforcing these shared professional beliefs and views.

One attribute of nearly all professional education is an academic focus on technology, rather than on relationships or service. Even though most professionals have received substantial training in technical execution of their skills, very few have received effective training in how to relate their technical skill to a user or customer of their services. It's easy for professionals to allow the emphasis of their discipline to overshadow the importance of focusing on the real benefits that their discipline can bring to customers. In addition, many individuals select occupations in specific professions primarily because of inherent interest in the technology used, not because of the process of providing the fruits of that technology to customers.

Understandably, this strong element of academic training and career selection which reinforces technology enhancement is directly reflected in the culture of a service unit. For most members of a service unit, the primary source of daily interaction is their fellow professionals within their unit. They would obviously reinforce to each other the importance of maintaining professional standards and advancing their technology. The group would tend to band together to fend off others who might threaten these goals.

Such technical goals can become so powerful and so deep-seated that they actually become the *central theme* of the service unit culture. For example, it is not unusual to find an information systems group whose real (but unstated) goal is to build the computer systems with the most stimulating and advanced technology available. Achieving this goal can provide the departmental members with intellectual stimulation and challenge, as well as professional status and prestige. But many of the demands of supplying excellent service to customers do not reinforce this goal—many are even in direct conflict. Customer units want quick service and care little about the sophistication of the computer that produced it. Customer units want reliability of service but are not concerned with what creates that reliability.

Technology or Customer-Centered Information Systems

The information technology function within most organizations provides a good example of how an internal culture might be driven by its own technology vs. the needs of the customer. For years, major technology suppliers such as IBM have focused on "information architecture" as the way to address a firm's information needs. This approach had a strong and positive reception among technical advocates and information specialists. It matched their desire to carefully organize and integrate all parts of the complex information system within an organization and has become the focal element of the culture of many current information processing departments.

This approach, however, has not played as well with the internal customers (who are likely to be much less technical in their orientation and expertise). Managers are still getting most of their information from noncomputer sources, and many beautifully conceived information systems, upon implementation, fall far short of their anticipated impact or usage. An approach that is centered on information technology is severely limited in its effectiveness in addressing the information problems of real internal customers.

Thomas Davenport, Director of Research at Ernst & Young's Center for Information Technology and Strategy, has contrasted information technology cultures that focus on information architecture vs. those that are customer or human-centered as follows:

INFORMATION ARCHITECTURES	*HUMAN-CENTERED APPROACHES*
- Focus on computerized data	- Focus on broad information types
- Emphasize information provision	- Emphasize information use and sharing
- Assume permanence of solutions	- Assume transience of solutions
- Assume single meaning of terms	- Assume multiple meaning of terms
- Stop when design is done or when system is built	- Continue until desired behavior is achieved enterprise-wide
- Build enterprise-wide structures	- Build point-specific structures
- Assume compliance with policies	- Assume compliance is gained over time through influence
- Control users' information environments	- Let individuals design their own information environments

SOURCE: Thomas H. Davenport, "Saving IT's Soul: Human-Centered Information Management," *Harvard Business Review*, (March/April 1994), 119-131.

Customers want service people who are responsive to *their* needs and care little about their technical sophistication. For the customer, technology is desired only if it directly satisfies their needs.

Customers expressing their own needs can be seen as attacking the central technical values of the service unit. This causes the service group to rally behind the internal norms and resist the attacker. The defense can grow to consume so much energy that it leaves little available for active listening and for understanding the needs of the customer unit. Of course, the verbiage surrounding this defense is in terms of "maintenance of high standards," or "the need to be technologically prepared for the future." But the real motivator is the desire to reinforce the technically based culture. An internally driven culture is in direct conflict with customer needs and hobbles the internal service unit that is striving for excellence.

Poorly Defined Expectations/Poorly Measured Results

The surest and quickest way for a service unit to generate intense frustration and anger is to fail to meet the expectations of a customer. Service satisfaction is closely tied to the gap between *customer expectations and the perceptions of actual service received.* Effective service units aggressively strive to close that gap. Doing so starts with clear articulation of expectations and measurement of results.

The Hay Group conducted a survey of fifty corporate information systems departments and twenty-five purchasing departments in a variety of industrial, financial, and service companies, to search for factors that contribute to high internal customer satisfaction.[3] The information systems and purchasing departments that ranked high on service satisfaction had significantly better and more precise specifications regarding the service to be performed than did their less well-rated counterparts. These excelling internal service units have been able to do a substantially better job of helping generate a precise articulation of service expectations and of gaining agreement on those expectations with customer units. For these service units, the considerable investment in defining expectations and clarifying standards paid off strongly in service satisfaction.

Despite the clear evidence that time and energy spent on clarifying expectations improves customer unit relationships, a majority of internal service units grossly under-invest in doing it. What seems on the surface to be trivial and obvious, is actually a practical challenge that almost every unit treats much too lightly. Managers of the units that do invest fully in the clarification process admit that it is more involved than they initially thought. Fighting the notion that this is a trivial exercise is one of the biggest barriers to achieving internal service excellence.

Prior to actual service delivery, customer units normally are able to articulate only vague and general expectations about service. They have had little incentive or push to really explore the subtleties of their service expectations. But once service has been rendered, it becomes all too clear that it was unacceptable. They may be unable to clearly articulate what was acceptable, but can become quite articulate about what is not. Unfortunately, this sets up a dangerous pattern of complaint and defense with the views of each party based on prior expectations about service that are both unspecified and unreconciled. Responsibility for forcing the articulation of expectations and standards lies squarely with the internal service unit.

Service units that have been able to complete this negotiation with customers have been amazed at how it has transformed their relationship from one of advocacy, defensiveness, and conflict to one of mutual problem-solving and collaboration. Freed of the necessity to constantly defend and rebut, the internal service unit finds time to invest in improving service effectiveness and efficiency—and a new partner to help it do so.

Inefficient Service Offerings

In 1986, Wells Fargo purchased Crocker Bank in California. The service offerings of the two large banks were very different and needed to be reconciled into a single product set for the newly merged entity. Crocker's set of service products—checking, loans, investments, savings, etc.—was extensive and complex in that it provided many products to a wide range of target-market groups. Wells Fargo, by contrast, offered relatively few products to much larger aggregates of customers. A real opportunity now existed for Wells to acquire new products to augment their limited offerings.

Instead, Paul Hazen, the president of Wells, surprised the investment market with the announcement that essentially all former Crocker services would be dropped and that the emerging Wells Fargo would continue the old Wells product line. When questioned, Hazen pointed to the results of a detailed analysis that looked at the cost of complexity in service offerings. He observed that, "best can be the enemy of good" in the offering of customer services and that Wells was to remain "a highly efficient purveyor of a simple range of bank products." He cited the continual problems and high costs that Crocker had experienced by trying to offer and support such a complex service offering. Wells had opted for the much simpler and more easily supportable product set that would ensure dependable high quality and low cost. The cost of complexity was a major factor in the decision.

For internal service providers, considering the cost of complexity is essential. Customer units continually request customized and special services. A customer-sensitive service unit could eagerly comply and develop new capabilities to deliver these unique and varied services. The customers would be happy and the service unit would feel that it had done its job well. But even though both customers and service suppliers seem to get what they want in this transaction, increasing service complexity is an insidious step toward a higher-cost and less reliable service offering. This same act, repeated over years, builds a cost basis and maintenance problem that can eventually condemn the internal service unit to rendering poor and expensive service.

Responsiveness, costs, and reliability for a service unit are the product of a series of historical managerial decisions about complexity tradeoffs (see below). Unfortunately, these tradeoffs often are not recognized explicitly and made only by default. High responsiveness and customized services must be purchased with the currency of higher cost and lower reliability. An explicit strategic decision regarding the desired level of service complexity helps clarify required tactical actions for the service unit.

Service Complexity Options

High Service Complexity	*Low Service Complexity*
• Many customized services	• Fewer standardized services
• High responsiveness	• Lower responsiveness
• High cost	• Low cost
• Low reliability	• High reliability

Let's look at a large data processing operation as a useful example of how cost and reliability can be inadvertently undercut. Customer units often request customization of the basic mainframe software of the corporation. These requests are made without knowledge of technology, costs, timing, or other systems implications. The data processing organization is eager to render full service (and is stimulated by the technical challenge of offering new and different services), but meeting these requests involves revision of large externally purchased software packages. Each of these individual revisions makes sense, but the cumulative effect over time is software packages that are costly to upgrade (as new releases of program changes come from the software vender) requiring programmers to "wire around" all the customizations that have been made. Many large organizations have incurred such elevated software costs and decreased reliability through this approach that they have issued a universal "no changes" order to try to deal with it—an extreme but pointed move. A less severe and more efficient approach is to explicitly decide on the desired level of customization (i.e., the level of responsiveness to special customer requests) on an *a priori* basis. Then, the data processing provider can use this as reference to make the individual customization decisions, thereby keeping costs and reliability within the desired corporate framework.

The complexity of work systems increases over time. Service delivery processes are made up of several separate subsystems, each producing a part of the service product and contributing to the larger whole. Each existing work process or sub-system has been created for reasons that, at the time, seemed very appropriate. But, most of these subsystems were created separately and, when combined create unintended consequences in other subsystems. Further modifications were then added (increased complexity) to deal with these unforeseen defects. Each sub-system within an entire service unit could be subject to these sorts of revisions several times over the years. These unintended consequences for other subsystems were themselves "corrected" by adding still more complexity. In the resulting labyrinth, overall *process complexity* can be very high. Many elements exist simply to "smooth the system" and to compensate for other unintended consequences created by other parts of the system. These elements greatly increase complexity, but add nothing to customer value.

An insidious increase in process complexity can easily occur if a response to the discovery of errors is the addition of more checking processes and systems. This is often done in the mistaken belief that more checking causes more quality. However, clear evidence exists that the addition of more external quality checking systems reduces the perceived responsibility of the primary worker for personally ensuring high quality. In addition to being ineffective, this response creates a morass of process complexity that makes good service almost impossible.

The field of systems analysis provides another useful perspective on understanding process complexity. A premise exists that full control of any system is possible only when the number of possible actions that can be taken by the system controller ("managers," in the case of internal service units) exceeds the number of possible alternative behaviors that the system can exhibit (Ashby's Law of Requisite Variety). Simply put, in order for an organizational system to be "in control," the number of options and actions available to the managers or workers must exceed the number of possible alternative outcomes that the organization might produce. Obviously, the number of possible control actions available is somewhat limited, and not easily expanded. Therefore, the degree of system control is very directly linked to the amount of variety imbedded in the system through inherent complexity. The greater the number and variety of services and customization, the lower the control of the system and, consequently, the lower its reliability. Adding degrees of control is difficult so reliability must primarily be ensured by minimizing system complexity.

Being concerned about the cost of complexity does not mean that you're disregarding customer needs or expectations. But momentary customer wants may sometimes be quite different from underlying customer needs. Responding to short-term customer requests may actually drive up long-term costs and drive down long-term reliability. In the end, the internal service provider that is shackled to an inefficient service offering cannot deliver excellent service.

Putting Chapter Five Ideas to Work

Here are some specific questions to help promote thinking about how this material relates to your organization.

✓ How has each of the four causal forces acted in your situation to help create an internal service problem:
  • The apparent monopoly?
  • Internally driven culture?
  • Poorly defined expectations/poorly measured results?
  • Inefficient service offering?

✓ Which of these forces is acting most strongly as a negative in your situation?

✓ How have the causal forces acted to create a trap for your internal service organizations which undercuts their ability to offer cost-effective and reliable service?

✓ What positive pressures are active in your organization which have the effect of countering the negative causal forces? Could anything be done to strengthen the positive effect of these pressures?

Chapter 6

The Downward Spiral

Emergent Forces

The causal forces described in Chapter Five directly undermine internal service excellence but they also promote the emergence of additional negative forces. The two most common emergent forces are deteriorating trust and a defensive internal climate.

Deteriorating Trust

Service excellence depends on quality communication regarding service expectations and feedback on service given. Good communication, in turn, depends heavily on the existence of a climate of mutual openness and trust. Trust is built only through considerable effort and skill, and is extremely fragile. A low level of interdepartmental trust causes crucial communications to be distorted or blocked, thereby making excellence in internal service almost impossible.

For example, the finance department of a large manufacturer was having increasing difficulty with operating units in creating an effective annual corporate budget. The units were hiding data and distorting performance figures in ways that made the construction of a realistic operating budget impossible. An external consultant examined the situation and found that all line units distrusted what finance did with their information. They felt that finance had used information in past budgetary sessions to bludgeon them into accepting impossible goals. The trust was so low that the line units were trying to restrict finance by cutting them off from information. Only a major effort to examine how trust was destroyed and then to rebuild it opened finance again to the information that was vital to its success.

Building and maintaining a high-trust environment, whether in individual relationships or between large groups, is a difficult and demanding process. *Trust requires each party to be willing and able to presume competence and good intent in the actions of the other party.* All discussions and interactions within a true high-trust environment (both public statements and private discussions between individuals) will be permeated with an underlying presumption that the other party is basically competent to do their job, and has the good intent to do so.

The test of the existence of these presumptions occurs when data suddenly arises that indicates a problem between the parties. In a low-trust environment, each party will be quick to explain the cause of the problem as incompetence or ill intent by the other party. In a higher-trust climate, judgment regarding the cause of the problem will tend to be withheld pending the acquisition of more data. (Since the other party is presumed to have competence and good intent, the problem must have been caused by something else!)

The existence of these two basic presumptions sets the stage for a positive and productive trust climate. Unfortunately, the four causal forces discussed earlier can sorely test the willingness of the departments involved in the service encounter to retain those positive presumptions about the other. If this fragile state of trust is disturbed by any of the causal forces, then both the trust level and the resulting communications deteriorates. More and more time is spent on accusations and finger pointing—less and less on productive discussions about real service issues. The debilitating effect of deteriorating trust and communications can be a strong blow to service quality.

A Defensive Internal Climate

As internal service deteriorates the CEO hears complaints at an accelerating rate and becomes concerned about the organizational time and energy now being spent on these internal issues. The CFO starts seeing worrisome symptoms that indicate cost escalation and duplication. Outside the service unit others see the emerging problems and add their own concerns. Each external party channels these concerns back to the service unit itself, and the result is an increased pressure on the service unit to "fix it!"

The Use and Abuse of Power in Internal Service

Power is a crucial element to be managed well in internal service relationships. It shapes interactions and communications between service supplier and customer units more than almost any other factor.

An internal service unit can exert power over the customer unit by forcing it to wait for service or to accept whatever service is available (demonstrating subordination and control). One manager of a line unit saw this behavior as "nothing but a way to express their arrogance and their contempt for us. That's not right! I'm their customer." For him, this was a grating act of control and subjugation. But customer units subjected to this kind of power-based abuse look for their own ways of gaining and exerting power in return.

The customer unit can demonstrate power through excessive demands for service, threats to obtain service elsewhere, or public denigration of internal service competence. Chris Lee, managing editor of *Training* magazine has heard it put this way:

> "Insecure, power-hungry managers vie for the position of client. Those are the people who are going to take advantage of the idea that the customer is always right. They see it as a way to feather their own nests. They're insecure; they learn the system so they can control it by saying 'I'm the client.'"

If power use by either party becomes a dominant part of the interaction, the entire relationship moves to one based on the acquisition and exercise of power, not on mutual problem solving and partnership. Trust and communications deteriorate and conflict becomes personalized. The entire interaction climate changes for the worse.

But if power between the server and customer is fairly balanced and is not the dominant mode of interaction, the stage is set for a relationship that is mutually respectful and facilitates open communication and problem solving--critical ingredients in internal service excellence.

Source: Chris Lee, "The Customer," *Training* (July, 1991): pp. 21-26.

The service unit's likely reaction is to "circle the wagons" and form a defensive shield. The group can rally around the defense of the service team and its internal goals, leading to an us/them split. From the perspective of either party, one way to make *us* more unified and cohesive, is to make *them* more ominous and threatening. The actions and motives of the others can easily come to be seen as sinister and threatening. In this climate, customer comments and suggestions regarding service are treated with skepticism and suspicion. Complaints become charges that are to be refuted. And these actions simply further strain the customer communications and top management support that are essential to the service unit's ultimate success. It is easy to see how this defensiveness can be ignited; it is much tougher to see how it can be stopped.

Communications is the Casualty

Once trust deteriorates and a defensive internal climate is established, the quality and accuracy of communications between the internal service unit and its customers declines precipitously. As between individuals, communications between organizational units that do not trust each other and feel defensive are dominated by attempts to protect oneself and to attribute blame to others. This understandable focus diverts energy from the solicitation and understanding of needed information from the other party. As a result, both the amount and accuracy of communications between units decline. This, in turn, sets up other negative forces that create a deadly downward spiral.

The Disastrous Interaction of Forces

While each of the individual causal and emergent forces has a powerful effect, the combination of them has a massive impact on the climate and production of internal service. Most often, the lack of clarity concerning expectations is what initially launches this crisis. The line unit becomes frustrated by what it sees as poor service and a lack of understanding of its needs. It complains to the service unit which responds by defending its performance. The service unit may feel that the appropriate service was supplied, or that the customer unit's expectations were unreasonable, or the service unit may know that service was not supplied for reasons beyond its control. Regardless of the reason, the line unit becomes increasingly frustrated with what they see as the service unit's insensitivity and inadequacy in meeting their needs. The line unit resolves not to "lose" the next one. It quietly sets up mechanisms to provide additional data and support for future claims of poor service (a great organizational "gotcha!"). The stage is now set for escalating conflict. The customer unit may try to appeal to higher authority or to enlist the support of other units to pressure the service unit. Both units see themselves as "victim." The diagram on the next page illustrates this unfortunate series of events.

The Degenerative Internal Service Scenario

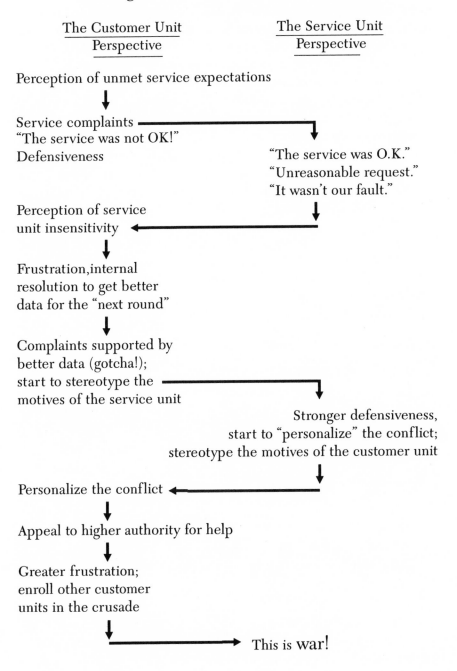

The Customer Unit
Perspective

The Service Unit
Perspective

Perception of unmet service expectations

Service complaints
"The service was not OK!"
Defensiveness

"The service was O.K."
"Unreasonable request."
"It wasn't our fault."

Perception of service
unit insensitivity

Frustration, internal
resolution to get better
data for the "next round"

Complaints supported by
better data (gotcha!);
start to stereotype the
motives of the service unit

Stronger defensiveness,
start to "personalize" the conflict;
stereotype the motives of the customer unit

Personalize the conflict

Appeal to higher authority for help

Greater frustration;
enroll other customer
units in the crusade

This is war!

By this time, the conflict has escalated beyond an interaction based on actual business data and has become very personalized. Each group tends to generate and reinforce internal group beliefs about what motivates the other group. The customer group starts to see the service group as uncaring, as only interested in their own internal processes, and as not sensitive to us, the customer. The service group, on the other hand, starts to see the customer group as unreasonable, as vindictive and not caring about the problems and constraints of the broader organization. Each unit is now able to find strong recurring evidence that reinforces their emerging negative stereotype of the other group. The conflict is absorbing an ever-increasing portion of company time and energy in efforts that have nothing to do with productivity or with satisfying the ultimate customer. The downward spiral continues.

The situation has become *locked in*. It has no chance of repairing itself. Only massive intervention can displace the destructive forces that have become embedded. The presence and effect of each of the debilitating forces is evident. Pain is everywhere. Frustration mounts. Everyone knows something has to be done, but what?

Revolution, Not Incrementalism

The forces that shape internal service performance permeate the entire fabric of the service unit. An assumption about a monopoly position, an internally driven culture, or a deteriorated trust and communications climate, are powerful and fundamental forces not subject to "quick fixes." Displacing a single force or factor will not result in lasting or significant change. Resistance to change of this magnitude cannot be overcome by nudging.

The needed change requires a major renaissance in the underlying assumptions that shape each interaction and communication. Successful change strategies must be based on confronting and revising the entire network of basic assumptions — in challenging and replacing them with a new set that is more aligned with service excellence.

Where Are We Going?

Understanding the debilitating forces at work in internal service environments prompts the question of how this understanding can be put into action. Throughout the remainder of this book, we will explore a very practical and effective process for moving from an awareness of the problem and forces that create and nurture it to the accomplishment of a performance turnaround. This process is comprised of four major steps. Each of these steps is the subject of a subsequent chapter and the group of them are combined into a process map for change that we will use as our overall guide through the turnaround process. The process map will be reviewed regularly to establish where we are in the overall process.

The Process Map
The Major Process Steps in Creating an Internal Service Performance Turnaround

1. *Assessment/Commitment*
   What is the overall nature and scope of this change—is this change what we want to do?

2. *Information gathering*
   What do we need to know to make this change successful?

3. *Action Planning*
   What specific changes need to be made?

4. *Implementation*
   How can people best put the planned changes into effect to create service excellence?

Putting Chapter Six Ideas to Work

Here are some specific questions to help promote thinking about how this material relates to your organization.

✓ What is the general state of trust and openness between internal service and customer units in your organization? If a problem occurs between them, is causation assumed to be incompetence and ill will or the opposite? What impact does deteriorated trust have on the quality of communications?

✓ What evidence do you see of a defensive climate in your internal service organizations? What impact does this have on the quality of communications?

✓ Does your organization have a predisposition toward piecemeal and incremental solutions to problems or does it generally move toward a more encompassing and complete solution? What could be done to move it more toward the latter in the case of attempting an internal service unit turnaround?

PART III
ASSESSMENT/COMMITMENT
How should we begin?

Introduction

Once you've identified the fact that a problem exists in an internal service unit, you're poised to take the next step toward a solution that will have real impact. You must now carefully assess the service situation and build a solid commitment to action.

Orient yourself with our position on the overall process map below and then we'll take another look at the Information Systems Division of Mid-Americorp.

The Process Map
The Major Process Steps in Creating an Internal Service Performance Turnaround

1. *Assessment/Commitment*
   What is the overall nature and scope of this change—is this change what we want to do?

2. *Information Gathering*
   What do we need to know to make this change successful?

3. *Action Planning*
   What specific changes need to be made?

4. *Implementation*
   How can people best put the planned changes into effect to create service excellence?

CASE: Mid-Americorp—Solidifying the Change Commitment

As complaints about the service of Mid-Americorp's Information Systems Division mounted, CEO Jonathan Greyson realized that action was needed. He knew that remedying the situation would require a solid organizational commitment to success.

But before he could rally the commitment and enthusiasm necessary to drive a turnaround within the division, he needed to assess the current situation carefully. He had to thoroughly understand the general factors that were creating the need to change as well as the details of the IS Division and its customer units. He conducted a detailed personal assessment of the situation by looking at major symptoms, performance outcomes, costs, and alternative actions. His analysis confirmed his suspicions about the depth of the problem and solidified his personal commitment to act.

Greyson approached David Rawls, head of the Information Systems Division, about his concerns. He knew that Rawls was frustrated by other bank units that didn't seem to appreciate the sophistication and technical excellence that his unit was striving to achieve. But Greyson was equally concerned with the impact a troubled systems division could have on the bank's bottom line. Greyson made clear his firm commitment to a major revision of the IS Division, though, and he wanted Rawls to head the turnaround effort. Rawls agreed, but it was obvious that he hadn't fully accepted the fact that something was seriously wrong with the IS Division.

In the meantime, Greyson was visited by three of his bank presidents who wanted to discuss what they termed, "a fantastic cost savings opportunity for Mid-Americorp." A Cleveland-based data processing company had proposed taking over total responsibility of Mid-Americorp's data processing function. The company would hire all of Mid-Americorp's present data processing employees as employees of its own, assume the financial obligations and ownership of the substantial hardware and software now run by the IS Division, and provide full services to Mid-Americorp for a fee. It estimated that it could save Mid-Americorp $2 million per year.

Greyson appreciated the chance to investigate a cost-savings opportunity for Mid-Americorp, but the promised savings were vague, and he wanted to take a stab at doing a real turnaround in the IS Division before deciding on outsourcing the service. He confirmed that he felt a significant reform of the IS Division was now necessary and asked the presidents to work with him to enroll the other presidents as cooperative partners in this important process.

Two weeks later, Rawls presented a plan for change to Greyson. His plan consisted of minor internal procedural changes or ways for the customer units to do a better job of requesting work. Greyson quickly pointed out the discrepancy between the severity of the IS problem as he saw it and the timidity of the proposed solution. He asked Rawls to attempt formulating another plan but Rawls decided it would be wiser for him to resign. He pointed out that his vision of the IS Division's function was clearly quite different from Greyson's and he had decided to submit his resignation rather than lead an effort in which he did not believe. Greyson was not totally surprised. He thanked Rawls for his generous service to Mid-Americorp and accepted his resignation.

Greyson's thoughts then turned to a successor for Rawls. He had always had doubts that Rawls would be able to separate himself enough from the unit he had built, to effectivly lead a real and substantial change effort. He knew that he could not lead the change effort himself since it would be at least a full-time job. He turned to Bill Walker who had joined Mid-Americorp eighteen years ago just out of college. Bill had worked in various capacities in a number of Mid-Americorp departments over the years, including several years as manager of a major IS department. Currently, he was head of the bank's retail division, responsible for all bank branches.

Walker was not the technical strongman that Rawls had been, but he knew the IS Division and he seemed to have earned the respect of its managers and staff. Plus, in working with the bank branches, he understood the importance of satisfying customer needs. Walker enthusiastically agreed to take over the IS Division and mange the change process. But first he would take two weeks to develop his thoughts about the change process.

Walker felt that a successful change effort would be rooted in cultivating behaviors, attitudes, and expectations that facilitated change. He first identified the desired behaviors of the customer units, the CEO, and the personnel of the IS Division—the way he would like to be. Clarifying his behavioral goals helped him visualize what he needed to do.

The Customer Units

The ideal customer unit would hold judgments and expectations in abeyance. It would cooperate as a partner in establishing procedures and service standards and in implementing improvements to service for the good of its performance as well as the overall organization. It would support the idea that a strong, productive relationship could always exist between it and the internal service unit. Ultimately, the customer unit will automatically assume that the service unit is competent, and has good intent.

The CEO

The ideal CEO would allow for deviations from the past and would commit the necessary resources to support the change and maintain high standards in service output. He would encourage others, particularly the customer units, to cooperate in the change process. He would act as a facilitator, overseeing the change process and ensuring that a power struggle does not ensue. Ultimately, he will consider the service unit to be a competent contributor to overall organization objectives.

The Internal Service Unit

The ideal internal service unit would be motivated to leave the status quo behind by accepting new ways of doing things and taking risks. Its focus is the customer. It would initiate continuous internal improvements that reflect its desire to satisfy the customer and would develop a cost/value sensitivity. Ultimately, it would be a reliable, respected supplier of services to valued customers.

Walker then interviewed various managers, including Greyson, and employees throughout Mid-Americorp regarding their views of the IS Division. He also solicited information from those within the IS division.

His interviews clarified the concerns of various parties. The customer units felt that they were getting poor service, were being treated unfairly, and were being overcharged for IS services. The CEO and senior executives expressed strong concern about the high-cost profile of the division and the exorbitant amount of time and energy that the conflict surrounding the division was wasting. IS Division personnel felt beleaguered and unappreciated. Morale had sunk to a frighening low.

From his interviews with the customer units, Greyson, and IS personnel, Walker realized that the current behaviors, attitudes, and expectations were quite different from what was desired. He assessed that a plan for change would have to be based on initiatives that would narrow the gap between the existing and desired behaviors.

Its success would depend on the commitment of all parties involved to rectify the service problem. Walker moved ahead with the first stage by immediately meeting with top managers within the IS Division. This was where the change process would be launched and Walker wanted to further assess their willingness and capability to change. He found some IS managers to be very reluctant, even hostile, toward change. Others were extremely enthusiastic and delighted that the needed changes were finally going to occur.

Walker organized another meeting with senior line managers from throughout Mid-Americorp, the "customers" of the IS Division. He announced that changes were going to occur within the IS Division—changes that would improve the service they were receiving—and that they were invited to participate in the process. As long as they were involved in the turnaround and saw positive results, they could be counted on as change partners.

The commitment from Greyson and other top executives was high as well. They pledged support and the needed resources to turn around the IS Division. The internal service unit renaissance was off to a strong start.

Putting Chapter Seven Ideas to Work

Here are some specific questions to help promote thinking about how this material relates to your organization.

✓ What external opportunities exist for your organization similar to those presented by the outside servicing proposal in Mid-Americorp?

✓ What would be the types of "desired behaviors" for customer units, the CEO, and the internal service unit if internal service systems were working perfectly in your organization? How far are these from current practice and experience?

✓ What specific groups of people in your organization would need to be brought "on board" to any major internal service unit turnaround effort?

Chapter 8

The Assessment/Commitment Process

Creating a solid foundation for an internal service turnaround requires developing and focusing the commitment of internal unit personnel, customers, and top-level managers. There are five steps in the assessment/commitment stage:

- Situational assessment
- Enrollment of top management
- Enrollment of leaders in the target unit
- Enrollment of key customer leaders
- Final commitment

Situational Assessment

In the turnaround of a troubled internal service unit, an analysis of the situation must be completed to determine the need for change, the extent of changes, and the capability of the parties involved to embrace the change. Success in organizational change requires advance identification of potential blockages and the construction of a solid change plan. The data which will be the foundation of this change plan are provided through a well thought-out situational assessment process which explores the general need for change as well as change related details of the internal service unit and its customer units. The Change Assessment Checklist identifies the major issues that need to be addressed in such an analysis.

Change Assessment Checklist

The General Need

- What are the major symptoms (such as user service complaints, high costs, poor coordination, duplicated services, etc.) that indicate a problem exists?

- Exactly which internal service units are most central to these symptoms?

- Which customer units are most impacted by service from these service units? Are these the same units that are now in the most "pain"?

- Which other organizational units or entities (not customers of the service unit in question) are exhibiting symptoms and concerns?

- How severe is the overall level of concern being expressed by outsiders?

- What is the value of the service? Is it worth fixing?

The Service Unit

(Choose one service unit for this analysis. Repeat for others.)

- What is the organizational boundary within the service unit that seems to cause most of the concern from others? (The entire unit? Subcomponents of the unit? One individual? One attitude?)

- What is the perspective of the service unit members and leadership regarding the severity of the problems?

- What is the perspective of the service unit members and leadership regarding the cause of these problems?

- How much pain is being felt inside the service unit because of these problems?

- How strong is the feeling within the service unit that changes are needed inside the unit itself? That changes are needed elsewhere?

- How much of the culture of the internal service unit is based on fostering and promoting goals which are internal to the professional or technical needs of the unit?

- How sensitive is the service unit culture to the needs of its customer units?

- How well does the internal service unit define service expectations and measure service effectiveness?

- How much are service standards and measures a matter of joint determination by customer units and the service unit?

- How is productivity and cost measured?

The Customer Units

(Segregate or cluster responses by customer units as necessary)

- What specific types of concerns are expressed regarding internal service received?

- How severe is the "pain" felt by this customer unit regarding service received?

- How substantially does the perceived service deficiency impact the ability of the customer unit to execute its task? In what specific ways? How much does it impact the out comes of the company as a whole? What is the overall value of the service rendered?

- What is the perception inside the customer unit regarding the cause of the service deficiency?

- How willing is the customer unit to be a supporting partner in a full-scale service turnaround with the service unit?

- What problems in the customer unit will be relieved by the resolution of the service unit problems?

- What problems in the customer unit might be exacerbated by resolution of the service unit problems? (If the service unit issues are being used by the customer unit as an excuse for performance shortfalls that really are caused by issues that lie within the customer unit, solution of the service unit issues will bring a new and unwelcome focus on the problems of the customer unit itself.)

Determination of the specific behaviors that are desired from various key people in the change effort can provide important early directional guidance. The types of behaviors that might be helpful are described below.

Enrollment of Top Management

Any significant organizational change demands substantial commitment of resources and cooperation of others. Continued top management support is essential to gaining necessary project resources and cooperation, and to overcoming the obstacles that will arise. The CEO and other top managers need a clear idea of the need for change, the process map to be used, the expected results, the timetable, and the required resources.

Key executives are busy and you may be tempted to quickly explain the changes, gain surface agreement, and move on to implementing the change. But this will lead to unrealistic expectations and to little familiarity with the real challenges involved. Many projects fail due to shortcuts taken at this point. The change process will require a major investment of time and energy for the organization. Top management wants maximum return on that investment. That's why they must fully understand the extent of the change process and its ramifications on current operations and fully support its implementation.

Enrollment of Leaders in the Service Unit

The choice of internal leadership for the change process is key to the success of an internal service unit turnaround. Individuals both inside and outside the service unit will arrive at conclusions about the real desired results of the change project by looking at who is chosen to lead the effort.

Enrolling key internal service unit managers and influence leaders in the change effort is a sensitive process. You must be aware that many of them were involved in creating and maintaining the mechanisms and processes that are now coming under such criticism. On the other hand, these key people are experiencing substantial pain in dealing with their internal customers. Life is far from pleasant for them. They have much to gain through dramatically improved unit performance. If they become convinced that a set of actions would

WHAT BEHAVIORS ARE NEEDED?

The Desired Behaviors of Key People that Are
Needed to Facilitate Change Process Success

	The Customer Units	The CEO	The Internal Service Personnel
DESIRED INITIAL BEHAVIOR	- Hold judgments and expectations in abeyance (those based on negative history - Cooperate as a partner in the process of setting up the expectations and service standards - Share a vision of a possible future that incorporates good service and good relationships with us (believe that it is possible!)	- Allow resources and deviations from history - Encourage others (particularly customers) to cooperate with this change process - Stay in reserve to balance power (if needed)	- Be motivated to do better (leave status quo behind) - Be willing to take a chance by shifting to a customer focus - Be willing to look at all issues in a new light. (Nothing is justified by "that's the way we always did it!")
MOTIVATION TO COOPERATE	- The hope that good service and good relationships will result	- The hope that the "service problem" will be eliminated	- The need to eliminate the present "pain"
DESIRED FINAL BEHAVIOR	- Work as a partner in helping to continuously improve service delivered to them - Strive for objectivity and a nonaccusatory relationship	- Support high standards for the service unit output - Act as a facilitator to help all parties use power well	- Initiate continuous internal improvement - Obsessive focus on customer needs
ULTIMATE RELATION-SHIP	- Automatically, in any trans-action, assume that the service unit is both competent, and has good intent	- See the service unit as a competent contrib-utor to overall company objectives	- Perform as a competent and respected supplier of services to valued clients

remove their problems and provide solid departmental functioning, they can overcome the initial inherent reservation about change and become enthusiastic participants.

Begin this enrollment process with a meeting of the senior managers of the service unit. Focus on three key areas:

- The need for change
- A vision of the future internal service unit
- Concerns and feelings about the change

Begin the session with a clear focus on the need for change coupled with a personal pitch by the CEO emphasizing the need. Keep the group focused on the need for change and allow all viewpoints, reservations, and suggestions to be thoroughly aired. Talk about the symptoms that indicate the need for change.

Be careful not to let the group simply lament the present state. And, keep the meeting focused on the issues that the group can control. The team must emerge with confidence that it can control its own destiny and has the commitment to do so.

When a common view of the need to change has been forged, move into a discussion of what the situation would be like if the climate and problems were corrected. Focus the group on the benefits of solving the problem, not on the difficult issues involved in accomplishing the change. This process helps individuals specifically identify potential benefits to them that would accrue if the problems were addressed and fixed.

By the end of the meeting, the group should have a full understanding of the need for change, and have had an opportunity to express concerns and reservations. In addition, the team should have visualized what an improved condition would be like. The group should *not* proceed into planning the change at this time.

You may also want to conduct individual and private interviews with key members of the group. These personal conversations are effective in identifying the various threats that individuals see in the change situation.

Everyone who is a member of the leadership team must be fully enrolled in the change process before it is launched. Change processes cannot survive continuing attacks from within the team by individuals who never agreed with the need for change.

The Dawn of Quality Focus at Xerox

In 1959, Xerox introduced the 914 plain paper copier and quickly revolutionized the entire document reproduction industry. For Xerox, this fantastic success launched an era of feverish growth and success. The company could sell all that it could make and became the youngest company ever to reach $1 billion in sales. In the mid-1970s, return on equity was steady at 25% and the company enjoyed an 80% market share.

But this heady success drove a company which was technology driven even further from its customers. During the 1970s, Japanese copier makers had targeted the U.S. market but were beginning small and were largely ignored by Xerox. The Japanese offered a small "desktop" copier that did get a good public reception, but was dismissed by Xerox as "flimsy" (the lightest Xerox copier at that time weighed 2,000 pounds). Two decades of dramatic success had insulated Xerox from customers and competitors.

But by 1980, the crisis had become apparent within Xerox. Return on equity was down to 6% and the formerly dominant market share was low and getting lower each month. Profits had slipped to 50% of prior years. Competitive checks revealed that the Japanese could sell a copier in the United States for less than it would cost Xerox just to manufacture it! It became obvious that things were bad and getting much worse at a very rapid pace. Substantial and very quick action was needed if the company was going to be rescued from a future of obscurity and ineffectiveness.

In 1980, Xerox launched a major "remaking" of the corporation. It began the process of competitive benchmarking to establish where competitors were on important productivity dimensions. Benchmarking provided the realization of the strong need to change as well as some of the specific directions of change. The organization was revamped into quality teams that examined the work processes in detail and were empowered to revise them. The entire Xerox work culture was rebuilt around the quality theme.

By 1985, these programs had stopped the Xerox fall in market position and returned Xerox to competitive parity. By the late 1980s, Xerox had regained competitive leadership and in 1989 it won the coveted Malcolm Baldrige National Quality Award.

SOURCE: Presentation by Kerney Leday, Regional VP, Xerox, Dec. 5, 1990, Houston, Texas.

Enrollment of Key Customer Leaders

You'll find that customer units are the easiest to enroll in the internal service unit turnaround. They have felt the need for change longer than anyone, and may be at a point of supreme frustration in their own efforts to remedy the situation.

Launch the change process for these key customer unit individuals through an initial session covering the need for change and a broad sketch of the anticipated process. Use this meeting to describe the crucial role customers will play and highlight specific requests for their cooperation.

One of the most important results of this meeting with customer unit managers is to change the fundamental nature of the ongoing interactions between the units. Deal directly with the anger and frustration that has resulted from past negative interactions with the internal service unit. Although this anger is now an irrelevant artifact of the past, it is still very real to the individuals in the customer units. For them it dominates the overall tone of the relationship between the two units. Replace this attitude with a cooperative climate based on partnership and mutual benefit. Recognition of the existence and reality of the anger resulting from poor service is crucial to converting the relationship into a positive partnership. The anger needs to be recognized, but not validated in these interactions.

Convince customer unit leaders that the change is real and is backed by serious and substantial effort and good intent. Provide specific evidence that allows them to look beyond past patterns of interaction and to gain a firm understanding of their key role in building the new, cooperative climate.

Help the customer leaders emerge from this initial change process encounter with an understanding of the role that they played in contributing to the current situation. Primary blame and responsibility rests with the internal service unit itself, but positive movement requires that the customer managers see their own demands for unnecessary or special service as unrealistic and detrimental to a successful turnaround.

Keep the customer units informed of progress throughout the entire change process to ensure their continued support.

Final Committment

Review the disposition of all key stakeholders as the last checkpoint before moving to final public commitment to the change project. Stakeholders include those who have a special interest in, or power over, the change process (e.g., the CEO, other top managers, customer unit managers, the management team of the internal service unit, etc.). This process confirms that a sufficiently broad commitment to the process exists and is commonly understood by all key players.

I Can't Fix 'All Screwed Up'

Many internal service situations deteriorate to the point that customer units are vocalizing their strident complaints about poor service in very general and emotion-laden terms. They cry that service is "all screwed up" and surround their complaints with equally general and loaded verbiage.

James C. Granier, Senior Vice President of First Commerce Corporation in New Orleans, is highly experienced in the practical variables that must be part of an internal service turnaround situation. Granier points out that it is up to the internal service unit to get beyond these vague and cathartic accusations. He contends that, "the truth is in the details." The conversation about service must not reside at a high abstraction level, but must forcibly drive to the specifics. Questions like: "Exactly what symptoms do you see that indicate inadequate service?", and "Precisely what variables are how far out of tolerance for how long?" Pursue these answers until the real truth about a particular service malfunction is uncovered, Granier suggests.

Absorbing the emotional content of a discourse with a customer unit that feels it has received poor service is challenging. But until the conversation has been drained of some of this strident emotion, little useful data about the malfunction is likely to be found. Executing a productive questioning process without appearing defensive requires considerable behavioral skill. In addition, the internal service unit must be sure that it is able to get beyond the normal defensive reaction and into a genuine scientific search for the real data. Skill at this type of interaction with customer units is vital for internal service units hoping to improve real service since reliable and relevant data is absolutely necessary to get beyond trying to fix "all screwed up."

Once an informal consensus has emerged from this first stage, a final formal articulation of the understood agreement can be documented and agreed upon explicitly. It should be structured something like this:

Description of the Need

- Why is this change being undertaken?
- What is the primary need being addressed?
- How do various parties see the need?
- What result is expected if the need is met?

The Situation

- What is the nature and extent of top management support for this change?
- What is the commitment by others (particularly the customer units) to the success of this change?

- What is the commitment by the internal service unit to the success of this change process?
- What is the support role for others in this change (top management, customer units, others)?

The Change

- What is the scope and nature of the change?
- What is the expected general process of the change (the process map)?
- What obstacles to successful change might be anticipated?
- What resources are expected to be needed?
- Who is responsible for the success of the change process? What authority and resources do they have?
- What is the general schedule of events and anticipated results?
- What are the expected results of the change?
- How will we know if we were successful?

Only if this detail is made explicit in advance, and agreed upon by all key stakeholders, will it have the needed impact on behavior. Everyone needs to understand the costs of the change, the real need for persistence and follow through, and the anticipated benefits. Be frank, open, and candid about the temporary hardships such a change process may entail. This agreement will serve as the groundwork for all subsequent change actions and must be complete and straightforward.

These steps provide the vital assessment and commitment that is required in a successful internal service unit turnaround. Each of the remaining three stages (information gathering, action planning, and implementation) is the subject of a subsequent chapter. Before we move on to the information-gathering stage, it might be helpful to look at the specific tasks that the change team must accomplish.

Task List for the Change Team

1. *Organize the team.* Assemble a change team to manage and push the project. Develop the internal processes and procedures that will be needed for smooth and speedy functioning.
2. *Solidify the need to improve.* Identify all key stakeholders in the change process and help them feel a common and strong sense of the benefits of a better service situation and of the need to change. Don't forget to keep the feeling of need within the change team itself solid and uniform!
3. *Obtain/analyze information.* Conduct serious introspection within the internal service department itself; how does it see itself? How does it do its work? How does it see its role and its customers. Gather and evaluate data from customers and other key stakeholders about how they see the department and its functioning.
4. *Clarify/revise the mission and role.* Considerable work must be done to carefully examine the present and the desired mission and role of the service unit. In most cases, a new, carefully crafted vision of the unit needs to emerge through this process.
5. *Devise a change plan.* An effective internal organizational change plan must be constructed based on the overall need to change, the new mission and role, and the data gathered from introspection and others.
6. *Execute the change.* The actual changes themselves must be carefully managed in a timely but effective manner.
7. *Build in continuous improvement.* The unit must have mechanisms that allow it to continuously learn and change by gathering appropriate performance feedback and adjusting itself and its services to the ever-changing situation.

Putting Chapter Eight Ideas to Work

Here are questions to help promote thinking about how this material relates to your organization.

✓ In your organization, who could/should act as the major driver or change agent behind a full rebuilding of the relevant internal service unit(s)?

✓ How would you respond to the questions in the "Change Assessment Outline"?

✓ What are the major issues and challenges in getting the top management of your organization fully enrolled in the process of renovating the internal service unit?

✓ What are the major issues and challenges in getting the leaders of the internal service unit on board with this coming change process? How would you accomplish this?

✓ How should the key managers in your customer units be involved in the initial stages of this change process?

✓ In your organization, what approvals or endorsements constitute a final go-ahead and a firm commitment to see this project through to a successful completion?

PART IV
INFORMATION GATHERING

What information is needed to guide a successful turnaround?

Introduction

Once you've assessed the internal service problem and rallied commitment from all affected parties, you will need information that will serve as the foundation for building an effective action plan. Some of this information lies in the assumptions and self-concepts of the internal service unit itself. Other information is in the needs and perceptions of the customer units, and still more is inherent in the processes performed by the internal service unit. In this part, we examine each of these important sources of data and how we can glean from them the valuable information that they hold. Review the process map and let's begin with a look at the developing situation at Mid-Americorp.

The Process Map
The Major Process Steps in Creating an Internal Service Performance Turnaround

1. *Assessment/Commitment*
   What is the overall nature and scope of this change—is this change what we want to do?

2. *Information Gathering*
   What do we need to know to make this change successful?

3. *Action Planning*
   What specific changes need to be made?

4. *Implementation*
   How can people best put the planned changes into effect to create service excellence?

CASE: Mid-Americorp —
Building the Foundation

Bill Walker, the new head of the Information Systems Division of Mid-Americorp, produced a process map outlining the general steps for the turnaround of his unit. He then needed to get the information upon which to build a detailed and effective operational plan.

Walker had to move quickly to take advantage of the positive, but fragile, climate that he had established through initial conversations with customers and stakeholders. Announcement of his appointment to head the division had created expectations for change that would not remain unsatisfied for long. CEO Jonathan Greyson was supportive, but had emphasized that strong corporate earnings improvements depended on a successful turnaround. Walker heard the clock ticking!

In his preliminary examination of the IS Division, Walker found that it expended a great deal of time and intellectual energy on honing technology and building and monitoring compliance with internal procedures. He recognized that change efforts had to focus on replacing the division's preoccupation with technology and procedures with a real passion for identifying and meeting customer unit needs.

With this goal in mind, Walker formulated a self-study process to be conducted by the division. The study was designed to give managers of the division deeper insights into the present state of the division. The managers needed to carefully and objectively examine the forces acting on the present situation, and to develop a shared understanding of the need for improvement. He organized a meeting of the IS senior managers to launch the self-study process.

It had been almost a month since the first meeting of the IS management team where Walker announced his plans for change. The tension in the group was apparent. Of the six senior managers in the IS Division, four had greeted the news of the impending change with obvious enthusiasm. The other two were not supportive of the process and failed to see the need to change. Walker wanted to use this meeting to enroll the more reluctant managers in the process.

The divisional self-study was launched with a one-day off-site meeting. Each manager filled out a brief survey about their perceptions of the division and its situation. They then discussed their collective answers to the survey questions. A minority felt that the division was doing fine, but that it was being targeted by difficult customer units and top corporate management. The problem, they believed, was with customer units and managers who made unreasonable requests and showed little appreciation for the service they received. But, the majority of views expressed reflected the high pain levels associated with interactions with customer units. After extensive discussion of the problem, the group agreed that a dramatic change was needed. They developed a list of action steps that are outlined below

Self-Study Action Steps

1. *Solidify the change team*. Specify the membership, goals, and timing of the team. The team develops a common vision of the problem and the need to change as well as its own specific internal work processes.

2. *Conduct analysis of existing work processes*. Conduct a detailed analysis of existing work processes that spans from initial customer need identification to final satisfaction and feedback.

3. *Identify customers and key agents*. Identify specific customer units and the key agents within those units that are most central to our services and can provide feedback that is representative of the entire unit. Also, identify other key executives whose viewpoints are crucial to the success of our unit.

4. *Prepare for solicitation of data.* Design specific survey and interview forms and gain support and participation information contributors. (Examples of specific forms are in Appendix A.)

5. *Survey customers.* Conduct a survey of customers regarding their service needs, expectations, and current level of satisfaction. This form (or a version of it) may also be used with our own internal people to gather comparison data.

6. *Conduct in-depth interviews.* Select key individuals for one-on-one interviews that will provide additional depth and insight. (Specific interview outlines are presented in Appendix A.)

7. *Assemble and analyze data.* Assemble and objectively analyze all of the information gathered in the self-study.

8. *Follow-up and "thanks."* Thank those who contributed input to the self-study and give them each a preliminary summary of the results of the study, and the general plan for future action.

The team launched a detailed analysis of the IS Division's current work processes. They gathered data on the various types of services requested and the specific way the division produced services to meet these requests. The team also gathered and analyzed the extensive set of procedure compliances that the division required of customer units.

The team spent a great deal of effort in precisely defining their customers and then identified individuals within each customer unit who could serve as proxies for that unit. Four individuals from each of the thirteen affiliate banks and ten people in headquarters departments were identified as key customer representatives. This was the cadre of people whose opinions and perspectives regarding IS service would be sought, and whose input would be viewed as representative of the customer base.

The team now felt a strong need to understand more about the perspective of these customers. A survey instrument would be used to solicit their perceptions regarding service needs, expectations, and current service. In addition, personal interviews with key people would be conducted by IS Division personnel to give deeper insights.

Data from the customer surveys and interviews confirmed the team's preliminary hypothesis that the IS Division had, indeed, been far too remote from its customers. Actual customer service expectations were far from what the team had predicted and the service now being rendered was viewed even more negatively than the team had feared. The gap between expectations and results was clearly a major contributor to many of the problems facing the division. The lack of agreement on standards and measures of service also emerged as a strong source of conflict. The need for substantial change was becoming even more apparent.

The IS team completed its analysis of the data and then constructed a final set of conclusions and observations about the present state of the IS Division and the need for change. The team's summary observations are presented on the next page. This information was assembled into a presentation for Greyson and customer unit managers. Greyson was very impressed with the objectivity and candor that the IS team had been able to exhibit in the analysis, and reiterated his continuing support of the process.

The customer information was also presented to all customer unit personnel who would serve as contact persons and as representatives of their units. They were pleasantly surprised by the insights and the frankness that the report represented. The IS team thanked them for their helpful input, and outlined the next stage of the change process, the construction of a plan to address the identified issues. It was clear to the customer unit personnel that a new day was dawning in possible relationships with the IS Division.

Summary Observations from Mid-Americorp Customer Unit Feedback

How is the Informations Systems Division Seen?

	BY ITSELF			BY CUSTOMERS		
	HI	MED	LOW	HI	MED	LOW
Understanding customer needs		X				X
Service quality	X					X
Cost-sensitivity		X				X
Responsiveness	X				X	
The need for change			X	X		

Largest Sources of Conflict/Disagreement

1. Unreconciled service expectations.

2. No agreed-upon service standards or measures.

3. IS personnel perceived as arrogant and aloof.

4. Low customer awareness of technical or cost limitations.

5. Low IS understanding of customer unit needs.

6. Poor "recovery" from service glitches.

7. An historic relationship dominated by hostility/conflict.

Some Positive Aspects

1. IS seen by all as very technically competent.

2. Both IS and customer units are eager to make things better.

3. IS now using these results to build an action plan.

Putting Chapter Nine Ideas to Work

Here are some specific questions to help promote thinking about how this material relates to your organization.

✓ How could a self-study such as the one conducted in Mid-Americorp be executed in your organization? How would it be structured? Who would participate? What would be the results?

✓ Where can your organization get expertise in organizational change technology? Does it exist internally? Are outside groups or individuals available who are knowledgeable and experienced in this kind of analysis?

✓ Would customer units in your organization, like those in Mid-Americorp, be willing and enthusiastic partners in the generation of data about internal service? What would need to be done to help insure their cooperation and contribution?

Introspection and Information

Once the need for change has been ignited it's hard to resist moving quickly into action to remedy the problem. A quick fix to cure the pain is tempting, but successful change efforts are based on solid action plans and solid action plans are built on detailed information. A primary task of the internal service unit striving to dramatically improve its effectiveness is to assemble a solid body of objective information that can serve as the basis for building such an action plan. This chapter addresses what type of data you should look for and where you will find it.

Conducting a Self-Study

An internal service problem cannot be solved with the same thinking that created it. Focus the self-study on gaining an understanding of the present state, not on how problems are going to get fixed. Pursuing action alternatives now would divert energy from the important task of gaining deep insights into the current situation. Your depth of understanding of the present internal service environment will keep you from reconstructing the unit in its own present image. The goals of the self-study are to:

1. Gain insights into the current situation.
2. Solidify and clarify the need for change.
3. Develop a common perspective on the problem.
4. Build information and insights needed for the change process, and
5. Foster the teambuilding and trust that will be needed.

Data-gathering efforts that address these goals can be accomplished by conducting a self-study that focuses on three areas:

- The service unit itself, and its culture, values, and perceptions
- The customer unit and its expectations and perceptions of service
- The work processes and procedures the service unit utilizes to deliver its service

Let's look more closely at what information can be obtained from each area.

How the Service Unit Sees Itself

How an internal service unit sees itself and its role in the broader organization largely determines where and how it seeks data that will be used in the change effort. If it sees itself primarily as a provider of technical excellence, it will look for sources of data on technical performance. If it sees itself as being driven by customer service needs, it will seek information from its customers and solicit their input and perspectives.

Therefore, the internal service unit should first undergo an internal survey—one that will generate initial information on the unit's perceptions of customers' needs, the quality and costs of services the unit delivers, and the needs for change. A sample internal survey which addresses these issues is included in Appendix A. That survey, adapted to your own organization can produce important information needed in the change process.

Generally, the service unit's internal investigation should focus on understanding the unit's:

- "Theory of internal service"
- Level of customer focus and awareness
- Segmentation of ownership
- Role in the overall organization

A *Theory of Internal Service*

Each organizational unit has a set of basic assumptions about itself and how it does its work—its "theory" of its business. Management philosopher Peter Drucker has described the "theory of the business" as a set of assumptions a business uses about its environment, mission, and required core competencies.[1] Many business failures can be attributed to a company's inability to keep its own theory of the business in line with changing needs. A solid theory of the business is consistent with the reality around it, is internally consistent, is understood by all key stakeholders, and is tested and revised continuously.

Similarly, an internal service unit that's striving to improve performance must examine and redefine its own theory of the business — more appropriately labeled its *theory of internal service*. Every internal service unit has a set of commonly understood beliefs and assumptions that determine how it goes about its work. These assumptions are based on how the unit sees its environment, how unit members see themselves, and how the unit sees its customers.

Significant improvements in unit performance are contingent on a candid examination of the fundamental assumptions that unit members hold. The change team can look at each of these assumptions as they exist today and also as they might exist in a "desired future state" of the unit. Questions a particular service unit might ask itself to provide insight into its own theory of internal service are:

How do we see our environment?

1. How is our unit seen by top management and by other key stakeholders?
2. What are the most important technologies for us?
3. In what ways are the demands on our unit stable and in what ways are they particularly dynamic?

How do we see ourselves?

1. What is the specific mission of our unit?
2. How does this mission fit with the overall goals and mission of the broader organization?
3. What is our role relative to other units in the organization? How do we view ownership of the elements of providng internal service?
4. What are the required core competencies for real excellence in providing our services?
5. How effective are we in providing services? How efficient are we in providing services?

How do we see our customers?

1. How much of our attention and energy is focused on identifying customer needs? How much is spent in determining how well the customer thinks we satisfied these needs?

2. How is power used in our relationship with customer units? How prominent is it in the relationship?
3. What priority do we give to customer needs as compared to our own internal technology and procedures?
4. How customer-driven would our customers say we are?

Candid answers to these questions build a clearer vision of a unit's real theory of internal service. Challenging that theory's appropriateness and effectiveness provides the change team with important new insights and possibilities.

Level of Customer Awareness

The internal service unit's culture serves as a source of information. Many service units have cultures centered on their own technology, or around compliance with their own production processes or procedures. Management consultant Karl Albrecht has noted the symptoms that emerge in a service unit that is driven by its own needs rather than those of its customer units. He suggests asking these questions of your unit:

- Does it try to force its customers to follow inconvenient procedures?
- Does it impose unnecessary paperwork burdens on its customers?
- Does it refuse to make people available for advice and assistance?
- Does it reject legitimate customer unit help requests?
- Does it try to push part of its own work load off onto its customers?
- Does it cut back on service levels in favor of its own internal resource needs?[2]

Infusion of a customer-driven ethic displaces this internal orientation. But to do that, the unit must recognize that it is not sufficiently customer-driven now. A candid challenge and assessment of the actual state of customer awareness for a service unit can be one of the most important elements of a self-study.

Take the Square D Co., one of the country's leading suppliers of electrical fixtures. CEO Jerre Stead realized that his company was technology and engineering-driven, rather than customer-driven:

"I believe more than ever in the need to let the customer define how you're doing. Square D has historically been recognized as a leading quality manufacturer. But when I came to the company two and a half years ago, profits were flat, market share was slipping slightly—gradually would be a better

The Apostles and Terrorists of Internal Service

Internal service customers are "captured." They usually have little choice about what service they use and how it is rendered. In a sense they are hostages to the internal service unit. A customer that feels such little control can easily become quite uncomfortable. This uncomfortableness can become explosive if added to perceptions of inadequate service.

In this situation customers can become quite extreme in their beliefs and behavior regarding the internal service unit itself. Thomas Jones and Earl Strasser have labeled these extreme customers *apostles* and *terrorists*. The apostles are those customers who have had such positive experiences with a service unit that they actively extol the virtues of the unit to others in the organization. They are the publicly active and visible outside supporters of the unit. The terrorists are those customers who have had such bad experiences with the service unit that they have become aggressive and public detractors of the unit. They seem to take every opportunity to point out any and all faults or failures of the unit. Unfortunately, the preachings of the terrorists can easily strike resonant chords in customers who may be relatively neutral but feel the anxiety of loss of control in their hostage role.

Intuit, the maker of the very popular Quicken software, is very focused on creating apostles among its customer group. Scott Cook, Intuit's Chairman of the Board, says "When you treat a customer so well that he or she goes out and tells five friends how great it is to own your product—that's when you're doing it right." Similarly, a goal for every internal service unit should be to create as many apostles as possible and both to convert terrorists and avoid creating them.

To do so requires careful attention and management. A detailed analysis of existing apostles and terrorists often reveals the incidents that caused their predisposition. For example, terrorists are frequently created through poor recovery from a service failure. Detection of a pattern of this behavior calls for strong service recovery improvement efforts in the internal service unit. This type of analysis and information is essential to successful change efforts.

Source: Thomas O. Jones and W. Earl Sasser, Jr., "Why Satisfied Customers Defect," *Harvard Business Review*, (November/December 1995), p.96.

word—and there was no growth in the company. But, we were still consistently number one in every product area. We had to move from an internal focus to an external focus. A lot of companies like ours fell into the trap over the years of doing things very well historically. We were comparing ourselves to ourselves year after year...so we set out to change our culture from an internal to an external focus."[3]

Just as companies such as Square D were forced to become much more driven by their customers, internal service units must become driven by the needs of their internal customers. Changing an internal service unit's culture to one that exhibits a high customer awareness is a difficult but necessary step in creating a renaissance within the internal service unit. Only a unit that sees the customer as central to all else will focus its information gathering in this arena.

Segmentation of Ownership

In gathering information from the service unit, you'll also want to look at *who owns what* in the service unit/customer relationship. This is a key determinant of how service is produced and where the service unit looks for improvement. In this context, the term "owned," means to take full responsibility for a portion or all of the interface between the service unit and customer. One very crucial distinction must be made and understood: *the customer's need is distinct from the means of meeting that need.*

- The customer unit must be the *owner of the service need* and is the ultimate judge of how well those needs are being satisfied.
- The internal service unit must be the *owner of the means of satisfying the need* and must be the competent expert in determining and employing resources and methods that will satisfy the customer's need.

In many deteriorating service situations, the distinction becomes muddied. The frustrated customer unit attempts to control the means for satisfying their needs and the service unit may try to dictate what the service need is. But if the internal service unit is not respectful of the customer unit's ownership of the need, or if it loses control of the means of need satisfaction, it is destined to operate as an incompetent and irresponsible servant—not as a respected partner. Being a partner implies *mutual* competence and contribution. The service unit is responsible for making sure that these elements of ownership remain clear. Look for indications of "who owns what" in the present situation as information is gathered.

Service Unit Roles

The internal service unit's role within the broader organization also provides valuable information for the self-study. Internal service units act in one or more of the roles outlined below. Successful execution of each of them requires different implementation strategies, different skills, and different approaches to customer units.

For example, a marketing department may be primarily charged with supporting field units (the support service provider). But they are also responsible for monitoring compliance with company-generated marketing programs (the franchisor). As interactions evolve, it is easy for the marketing department to allow focus and attention to drift to the more power-laden role of franchisor. In the support role, the marketers see themselves as subservient to the customer unit. But in the franchisor role, they call the shots, and they have the power. This is more fun and easier. Therefore, the marketing department may neglect its primary role as a support services provider. It's easy to see why such a shift would prompt resentment in the customer unit. What they feel they need is support, but what they are getting is domination. Your self-study needs to look closely at the match between the roles needed by your organization and the ones preferred or occupied by your service unit.

Roles of Internal Service Units

ROLE	*DESCRIPTION*
Support Services Provider:	In this capacity, the internal service unit (the supplier) is adding value through the services that it provides for other company units (the customers). Most of the activity of service units, such as information systems and purchasing, is geared toward providing support services.
Information Flow Manager:	In this role, the internal service unit facilitates the processing and flow of information between other company units and top management.
Franchisor:	Internal programs, products, or services may be developed and moved to the field units for action. However, some internal service units, such as R&D, engineering, and marketing, have considerable portions of their role devoted to the monitoring of this implementation and how the field units utilize their services. They also support the field units in this implementation.

| Overseer: | Some service units monitor compliance with certain desired processes or attainment of specific levels of performance. Most of the activity of an audit department, for example, is in this realm. A human resources department may occupy this role in regards to compliance with certain government regulations, and a finance or accounting group may play this role in regards to budget performance of various organizational units. |

The Customer Unit as a Source of Information

A customer unit is the source of some of the most crucial information needed by an internal service unit to plan and complete a service renaissance. The best companies spend enormous time and effort researching and studying their external customers. The best internal service units do the same with their internal customers.

Start the process by carefully determining exactly who the internal customers are and how you will get feedback and information from them—both as a part of the self-study and later to monitor actual service performance. This may sound simple, but it does require some careful thought. Build a comprehensive list of the services provided by the unit and identify the specific users of each service. When you've completed your list, select customer representatives from each user group who can provide information and feedback regarding service. These should be the individuals who have the greatest impact on decisions about service delivery, make judgments about the quality or adequacy of service delivery, and routinely interact with the service unit. Select two to five representatives from each customer unit who you think will represent the views of the entire customer unit.

In addition to clearly identifying who your customers are, you should determine the other key *stakeholders* in the service unit's performance. These are the constituencies whose support, input, and influence are critical to the ongoing success of the service unit—those who have a stake in the unit. The list would certainly include the CEO of the organization as well as other top-level executives.

Once you've identified the service unit's customers and key stakeholders, you must define the expectations, needs, and perceptions they have regarding the current level of service. Detailed surveys of customer units and stakeholders provide valuable data in the information gathering process. A sample survey is included in Appendix A. Such a survey delves into customer needs, service quality, cost sensitivity, responsiveness, and the need for change—all areas of information that the internal service unit must have if it is to build a successful action plan for improvement.

In addition to a written survey, you can gain deeper insight on the customer perspective through personal interviews with key customer representatives. A sample interview format is included in Appendix A. Most customers are more than willing to "open up" about their feelings concerning the performance of their suppliers, so use these interviews as a tool to provoke honest, thoughtful responses—it may be the first time anyone has asked them what they think. Focus your questions on positive and negative experiences, the customer's perceptions of the service unit, and the customer unit's needs vs. their expectations.

The specific objectives of the customer survey and interviews are:
- To provide greater understanding of the precise nature of the basic service needs of the customer unit
- To codify the specific current customer expectations regarding service
- To provide insight into the customers' views regarding the current state of service
- To confirm to both internal and external groups the importance of customer perceptions and viewpoints in creating the internal service unit renaissance

Let's look more closely at the information you can draw from analyzing customer perceptions and expectations. Customer satisfaction is a function of both the customer's prior expectations about service and their perceptions of the service that they do receive. The challenge for an internal service provider is to help the customer find credible reasons to look for improved service—and then to produce the service results to justify these higher expectations.

One way to more effectively analyze the customer's perception is to look at those interchanges that influence most the customer's view of the service they receive. Jan Carlzon, the CEO of Scandinavian Airlines System (SAS), has referred to these key interchanges as "moments of truth" for the customer. When Carlzon assumed leadership of SAS, it was structurally disorganized and struggling with an $8 million annual loss. He found the reason for the company's problems to be its inability to view its operations from the customers' perspective. Quite simply, SAS assumed it was in the business of flying airplanes as opposed to servicing the needs of the customer who flew in airplanes. It had become obsessed with its own technology and had an internally focused vision of its mission. The need to move to a more customer-centered approach was clear but the means to do it were murky.

Carlzon initiated a study that identified those specific interactions between SAS and its customers that served as the basis for their perceptions of the airline. By focusing on improving the quality and value of those specific interactions—identified as the "moments of truth"—SAS managed to achieve a remarkable turnaround. In two years, the company posted a $71 million profit and was voted airline of the year.

Clearly, it is important that an internal service unit understand its customers' perceptions and perspectives. However, many service units fail to realize the importance of managing the perception of the unit's performance. Internal improvements that fail to address other's perceptions of the changes will slow any progress in the internal service unit renaissance. The service unit must be able to make the right internal changes *and* positively influence others' perceptions of those changes.

Equally important to knowing your customers' perceptions is a thorough understanding of their expectations. Expectations are usually based on the customer unit's past experience with the service unit. Asked what kind of service they expect tomorrow, most customers will describe the type of service they received yesterday. For a service unit trying to break out of the mold and achieve a turnaround, this can have both a positive and a negative effect.

On the positive side, a poorly performing service unit may have driven expectations so low that almost any change will boost the perception of service delivered. On the negative side, a poor history of service only leads the customer to expect continuing negative performance.

Often, what appears as poor service is really a lack of clarity or practicality in the customer's service expectations. Internal customers who have never had to specifically articulate their service expectations usually are operating with a disorganized "wish list" that represents the type of services they expect. These services can be either financially imprudent or technically infeasible. The internal service unit needs to work with the customer to clearly define expectations.

It is during this interchange that the internal service unit can align customer service expectations with what can be provided practically and cost-effectively.

Working with the customer to define expectations helps distinguish between customer wants and actual needs. When asked what they *want* from the internal service unit, a customer unit may say they'd like infinite service diversity and highly responsive customization. They also *want* extremely high reliability and very low cost from the internal service unit. Such drastic requests inherently drive reliability down and costs up. Therefore, the internal service unit must be able to discriminate between what's desired and what's really necessary. Making this important distinction requires a good understanding of the competitive strategy of the entire organization. For example, if a company's strategy is to gain competitive advantage by being the low-cost supplier, then individual internal service units must align their strategies with that objective.

The Work Processes

The final element of an internal service unit self-study is a detailed construction and analysis of the existing work processes. This provides the information needed to devise changes in the work processes themselves.

To complete an analysis of work processes, first determine how service needs are identified. How is a service request made? From whom, and to whom? How is the service generated? How is it delivered? How is feedback solicited? How are processes revised?

Practical and effective tools exist that work groups can use to visualize work processes, find problems, and devise improvements. Some of these work process analysis tools are described below. Although the work analysis should begin immediately as a part of the self-study, it will need to be continued throughout the entire turnaround process as new questions emerge and the service offering is altered.

Work Process Analysis Tools

Flowchart: These are schematic pictures of the various steps in the work flow, presented in a linked network that represents the work order, sequence, and decision points. Particularly helpful in providing a complete picture of the overall processes which can then be used to direct more specific analysis.

Paretochart:	This is a series of bar charts representing the frequency or intensity of various actions or work events. Sometimes refereed to as an "ABC analysis," this is useful in identifying problems and finding sources of problems.
Cause/Effect Diagram:	Sometimes called a "fishbone diagram," this is a map of relationships or factors that impact a problem or issue. Particularly helpful in diagnosing tough problems.
Operational Definition:	Determining a precise set of definitions of what various work elements are and how they are to be measured can add needed clarity to murky situations.
Stratification Analysis:	This type of analysis divides or stratifies data in ways that can reveal underlying patterns which help in locating problem areas.
Time Plot:	Examination of how things change over time can reveal how introduction or removal of certain factors changed performance. A "control chart" is a time series plot with the overlay of "acceptable" boundaries or variation limits. Establishing these control limits is useful in determining when a service is within vs. outside acceptable bounds.
Scatter Diagram:	This two-dimensional graphical plot displays the relationship between two characteristics of the work process or results. It is especially effective at finding relationships and links between variables.

For a full description of these and other work analysis tools, see *The Team Handbook*, by Peter Scholtes, Joiner Associates Inc., Madison, WI, 1988.

Applying the Self-Study Data

Once you've gathered data through a comprehensive self-study, you'll want to extract information from the data on the following:

- How consistently and uniformly is the service unit viewed by various customer and stakeholder groups?
- How does the customer perspective reinforce or contradict the results of the internal service unit's survey?
- Are there common themes about present service?

- What are the biggest areas of "pain" for the customers? How does that relate to the sources of "pain" felt within the service unit itself?
- What is the size and nature of the gap between service expectations and service perceptions?
- What patterns exist among the perceptions of various types or ranks of customer representatives?
- Do perceived service problems seem to center more around initial service, or around service recovery (the actions taken immediately following a service problem)?
- What are the most defining moments of truth in the interaction with customers? You might use the data to answer some more speculative questions as well.
- What specific events of recent history might have contributed to these perceptions? (Be careful not to put value judgments on the perceptions—it is more productive to see perceptions as fact, not as right or wrong.)
- Are there incidents in the history of the relationship (mythical or real events) that have a high impact on day-to-day transactions?
- Specifically, how does the self-perception of the internal service unit differ from the perception that the customer has of it? (Resist the temptation to justify or validate the perceptions.) What might account for this difference?
- What factors inherent in the service unit processes or procedures might have contributed to the perceived service issues?
- What factors in the service unit culture might have contributed to the perceived service issues?

The team charged with leading the internal service unit renaissance must carefully examine the data and then present its conclusions and a plan of action to key stakeholders and customer representatives. Not only does this force the organization of a change plan, but it also opens the lines of communication between service supplier and customer. The service unit sees its customers as more "human" with real needs and expectations. The customer unit senses its input and opinions are truly valued by the service unit. This entire process contributes strongly to future positive relationships between the service unit and customers, and to the establishment of high-performance service delivery.

Putting Chapter Ten Ideas to Work

Here are questions to help promote thinking about how this material relates to your organization.

✓ What recent examples in your internal service unit history illustrate "customer-orientedness," or lack of it?

✓ What is the most powerful "central driver" of the internal service unit culture (technical excellence, high standards, self preservation, customer needs, etc.)?

✓ Which, if any, of the following symptoms of internally driven service units exist in your organization?

  • Does it try to force its customers to follow inconvenient procedures?

  • Does it impose unnecessary paperwork burdens on its customers?

  • Does it refuse to make people available for advice and assistance?

  • Does it reject legitimate customer unit help requests?

  • Does it try to push part of its own work load off onto its customers?

  • Does it cut back on service levels in favor of its own internal resource needs?

✓ In the present internal service unit/customer unit interface,

  • Who owns control of the definition of what the customer needs?

  • Who owns the means of determining how customer needs get satisfied?

PART V
BUILDING THE ACTION PLAN

How can an effective plan for change be constructed?

Introduction

Conducting a self-study should provide you with considerable insight and definition regarding key players, relationships, expectations, and processes—information needed to create a successful plan for turn-around. You'll use that information to build a plan of action. There are four steps in the building process:
- Creating a service strategy
- Devising service standards
- Revamping internal service operations
- Linking the plan to others

Review our position on the process map. Then we will rejoin the Information Systems Division of the Mid-Americorp as they create their plan of action.

The Process Map
The Major Process Steps in Creating an Internal Service Performance Turnaround

1. *Assessment/Commitment*
   What is the overall nature and scope of this change—is this change what we want to do?

2. *Information Gathering*
   What do we need to know to make this change successful?

3. *Action Planning*
   What specific changes need to be made?

4. *Implementation*
   How can people best put the planned changes into effect to create service excellence?

Chapter

CASE: Mid-Americorp—Action Planning

The change team for the IS Division at Mid-Americorp had embarked on an aggressive information-gathering project. They assembled the data from the customer and internal surveys, one-on-one interviews, and work process analysis for a three-day session in which they would develop a complete action plan. The first step was to devise a service strategy for the IS group. They hammered out the following statement of service strategy:

Satisfaction of the information-processing needs of its customer units is the primary goal of the Information Systems Division of Mid-Americorp. In meeting that goal, the division will take all needed initiative to:

- *Earn a position as a respected and equal professional partner with customer units.*
- *Maintain intimate familiarity with the information needs of its customers.*
- *Produce services that focus on customer value-added and that meet specific service delivery standards that are agreed-upon with customers.*
- *Monitor, measure, and present feedback on the division's service effectiveness to ourselves, customers, and top management.*
- *Contain costs and promote service reliability through standardization of service offerings wherever possible.*
- *Treat customer representatives with courtesy, respect, and professionalism.*

In defining the service strategy, the team realized it needed more customer insight and empathy before continuing, so key personnel of the IS Division were assigned to spend one week each working beside their primary customer unit contact person. This experience helped establish the basis for more open communications and understanding that would be needed as the change plan was developed. The team decided that three additional tasks needed to be completed:

1. Develop service standards.
2. Revamp internal operations.
3. Link the plan to others outside the unit.

Developing Service Standards

In developing service standards, the group chose to look at existing service discontent as a starting point. Feedback from customers and IS employees confirmed the wide variance in expectations about service, and in perceptions about the quality of service actually rendered. Even when discussing the same service event, perceptions were often so diverse that it was difficult for the team to believe that the same incident was being described.

Criteria, such as response time, system availability, and report accuracy, were subject to a wide range of interpretation of "good." Although many perceptions of service problems seemed to center on a lack of clear and early definition of expectations, others were precipitated by the lack of agreed-upon service measurements. Examining the details of service problems helped the team discover the various informal measures customer representatives used to judge good vs. bad service—measures that rarely aligned with the ones that the unit itself used to evaluate the quality of its work.

Based on this information, the team set out with the customer units to define the specific areas of service that were important. They also sought agreement on the level of acceptable performance in each area.

The process facilitated an in-depth discussion of all service expectations and provided the opportunity for the service unit to confront customers about inappropriate or inordinately expensive expectations.

They developed a set of service guidelines that were composed of ten quantitative standards and six qualitative ones.

This mix would allow precise measurement of some of the key aspects of service and provide for more subjective feedback as well. Each of the quantitative standards was composed of a dimension—the area to be measured—and a service level, or the expected amount of fulfillment of each dimension. The standards provided measures for various aspects of service timing and quality. Meeting all agreed-upon standards as described below would constitute "excellent service."

IS Performance Standards

Quantifiable Standards

Dimension	Service Level
1. Daily reports on time	100%
2. Daily reports correct on first delivery	99%
3. Four-second average mainframe peak period (12 noon–1 P.M.) response time	99%
4. On-line terminal availability (7:30-5:00)	98%
5. On-line files current at 7:30 A.M.	100%
6. ATM availability (percent of transactions processed on-line)	98%
7. Research reply time	
A) Copies of checks and statements within 24 hours	100%
B) Internal research and adjustments within three days	100%
8. Statements rendered within two days	100%
9. Cash letter deadlines met	99%
10. Systems development (programming) projects completed as scheduled	96%

Qualitative Measures
Monthly Subjective Ratings, Key Customer Reps
(1 = Poor, 10 = Excellent)
- A) Friendliness
- B) Speed of service
- C) Responsiveness
- D) Staff's level of knowledge
- E) Staff's ability to communicate effectively
- F) Accessibility of staff

It was agreed that monthly performance statistics would be distributed internally and to all customer representatives by the fourth working day of the next month. The team also developed a monthly follow-up mechanism to address areas of low ratings that might emerge. The IS people most influential in each standard area would personally contact customer representatives to inquire further about any service problem.

Revamping Internal Operations

The division needed work processes and internal operations that could deliver service that met the newly defined standards. To define those operations, the division continued an examination of the internal work processes which had begun in the information-gathering stage. It produced detailed flow charts of the existing processes and procedures by which work was now done in the division and chronicled many of the underlying assumptions that guided everyday work. This look at the existing systems detail revealed a mind-boggling complex of intertwined processes, procedures, and rules. Many processes seemed to exist primarily to offset the consequences of some other system process rather than to produce value added for the customer. Obviously, the systems had evolved in a piecemeal fashion.

A look at historical service offerings confirmed that over the years, the services offered had become highly customized and specialized and had been instituted to meet unique customer requests. The group analyzed present service offerings by classifying each "service event" (one delivery of one service to one client) of the last year as either standard or special. A standard service was a regular and uncustomized service, such as normal check processing or regular reports. Special services were customized or unique services, such as single-user reports or special processing actions. Data on the service quality problems over the last year (mostly complaints by customers) were then matched to each appropriate service event. As a final step, the group asked the Mid-Americorp accounting group to allocate costs to each type of service event. This Pareto analysis produced the following proportion of volume, quality, and cost attributable to standard vs. special IS services:

	Standard Services	Special Services
Volume		
% of IS work	82%	18%
Quality Problems		
% of quality problems	15%	85%
Cost		
% of IS costs	53%	47%

Although special services comprised only 18 percent of total service volume, they had become a major source of both service quality problems (85 percent) and costs (47 percent) within the division—the same two topics that had been the source of strong customer complaints!

Customers would not want to give up their customized services without very good reasons. As the team stratified current special IS services in more detail, they determined that for 20 percent of the current special services, the need had expired and the service could now be canceled. Another 31 percent were very similar to existing standard services and could be easily converted to standard services. Fifteen percent of the existing special services could be converted into a small number of new standard services and 34 percent needed to remain as special services.Through this process the team had reduced the number of special services by two thirds.

The group recommended that the customer units should be approached regarding the changes in status of certain services. The changes would result in lower overall costs and higher service reliability, they explained. The accounting department quantified the savings that could be anticipated from these changes. Customers could expect to be charged 10 percent less and errors could be cut by 40 percent if these changes were enacted.

The division's entire operation would need to be fundamentally revised to accommodate these changes.

Completing and Linking the Plan

The team integrated all parts of the plan into a coherent and clear document and reviewed it with Bill Walker and the managers of customer units. With only minor suggestions for revision the change plan was accepted for action. After what seemed an eternity of preparatory work, the IS Division was ready to undergo its renaissance.

Putting Chapter Eleven Ideas to Work

Here are some specific questions to help promote thinking about how this material relates to your organization.

✓ In your organization what elements already exist (mission statements, broad goals, or strategies) that might be used in devising a service stategy? How much experience has your organization had with thinking and planning at a strategic level?

✓ What could the major elements of a new service strategy be for your internal service unit? Which of these elements would require the most work to define and articulate?

✓ What has your organization's experience been with trying to set and use service standards? If it has been a negative history, what could you do to overcome this initial predisposition against such an effort?

Building an Effective Change Plan

What is a Change Plan?

Assessment provided the first look at the internal service problem and generated an organizational commitment to fix it. Additional research produced the foundation for the change. It is now time to turn to building the actual plan for the changes that will cause the desired performance turnaround. A large organization is complex and the process of changing it is even more complex. Therefore, a well thought-out and integrated plan is needed to guide the change process. The plan must address four main questions:

- What is the overall *service strategy* that provides direction for the plan?
- What *service standards* should be developed to guide, measure, and evaluate performance?
- What changes in *internal service processes* are needed to achieve new standards?
- What *links* need to be established between the internal change efforts and other parties?

Chapters Twelve and Thirteen are devoted to the exploration and resolution of these questions.

Creating a Service Strategy

An effective guiding vision for the internal service unit transforms a general and vague wish to "do better" into specific actions that launch a real performance turnaround. Developing a *service strategy* provides this framework for action. The strategy is simply a complete statement of the way that a particular service organization does its work. It takes into account the customers and their needs and the parameters the service unit uses to satisfy those needs. In particular, a well-developed service strategy answers the following questions:

- Exactly who is our customer, and what needs do they have that we are targeting for satisfaction?
- How can we add value—from our customer's point of view?
- What is our mix of service roles in relation to our customers (what types of functions do we serve)?
- What is our specific service offering (those critical services that will be our focus, and in which we will achieve excellence)?
- How should we handle the tradeoffs among service complexity, reliability, cost, technical currency, and responsiveness?

Once these questions have been answered, the results can be melded into an integrated overall service strategy statement that serves as a continuing reference in determining the remainder of the action plan.

Building a Vision of Excellence

A service strategy must be based on a vision of the specific character-istics that provide excellence in an internal service unit. The more specific the vision of excellence, the more pointed and effective the strategy can be. Figure 1 portrays four developmental stages that an internal service organization can experience. Locating the particular stage which best represents your own present development can pro-vide a vision of what is necessary for future excellence, thus helping direct growth, strategy, and planning.

The exciting challenge of an internal service turnaround is to move the troubled unit through these stages—decreasing conflict and in-creasing contribution as each new stage is achieved. These four stages of development provide a striking contrast in internal service matu-rity and effectiveness. Internal service units in stage one are unap-preciated and are caught in a swirl of conflict and recrimination which renders them ineffective. Stage two organizations are markedly bet-ter in performance, but still more focused on themselves than on their customers. They are seeing that service delivery must be managed, not just allowed to happen. Examples of stage three (emerging excel-lence) and stage four (world class internal service) are more rare. These

Figure 1   Stages of Internal Service Unit Development

Attributes	Stage 1 BELEAGUERED PROFESSIONALS	Stage 2 COMPETENT RESPONDER	Stage 3 EMERGING EXCELLENCE	Stage 4 WORLD CLASS INTERNAL SERVICE
SERVICE UNIT SELF-CONCEPT	Unappreciated, unjustly persecuted, highly professional	Skilled, unrecognized servant	Learning, improving, highly skilled	Excellent at identifying and meeting customer unit needs
CULTURAL DRIVER	Maximizes own technology, insulated from attack by "outsiders"	Own technology, reduce conflict	Needs of customer units	Needs of customer units
RELATIONSHIP WITH CUSTOMER UNITS	High advocacy, much conflict, anger, and frustration	Meets some customer expectations, blame-oriented problem-solving	Developing toward partnership, meets most customer expectations	Highly valued as a competent and respected partner
SEEN BY COMPANY AS	A severe cost and reliability problem	Low profile, not crucial to the business, low respect	A solid and competent contributor	A valued source of corporate competitive advantage
USE OF TECHNOLOGY	To maximize internal professionalism	To improve internal functioning	To better meet customer needs	Innovative in meeting customer needs and providing competitive advantage
PRIMARY ENERGY EXPENDITURES	Gaining better customer unit compliance with own internal procedures, coping with conflict	Smooth internal processes, meet customer demands	Anticipate customer needs, assure excellence in service delivery	Learning, innovation, improving competency and customer need insights

internal service units have shifted to a primary focus on the customer and are aspiring to real service excellence.

Development of a service strategy that provides practical and effective guidance requires a vision of the type of service unit that is desired. The change team must be able to deliberate and articulate the vision that they see as possible and desirable. Only then can the developing service strategy gain the needed clarity and direction.

Challenging the Fundamentals

The difficulty of developing a meaningful service strategy increases in direct proportion to the degree to which the basic fundamental premises and assumptions of the unit are challenged. Some of the basics of the existing processes are likely to be seriously flawed, and only a broad and objective look at the fundamentals can reveal this.

Reengineering, has emerged as a tool that utilizes this fundamental challenge. Reengineering focuses on challenging the basic concepts of *what is necessary to be done,* not on how existing processes can be improved. Attention shifts from "doing things right" to "doing the right thing." Reengineering gurus Michael Hammer and James Champy have suggested that "it is the fundamental rethinking and radical redesigning of business processes." It does not ask "what should we do better," but asks "why do we do that at all?" Reengineering sweeps out those institutions and processes that have evolved over the years to serve some initial, but now extinct, need or those created to patch over other, more basic problems.

Some reengineering success stories are impressive. Union Carbide, for example, used reengineering to save $400 million in fixed costs in three years. GTE and Blue Cross of Washington and Alaska claim 20 percent productivity increases through their reengineering efforts. But a full reengineering effort is a strong dose of organizational medicine that has devastated some organizations. Dismembering the entire organization chart may be too extreme in many cases, but challenging the fundamentals is not.

Conduct a fundamental reexamination of basics with a primary focus on the customer to prevent your cost-cutting efforts from becoming myopic and internally focused. If ultimate customer effectiveness is diminished, the savings are false. Analytical skill, candor, and considerable insight are required to evaluate the fundamental premises behind how things are done now. Challenging the funda-

The Integration/Differentiation Quest

Paul Lawrence and Jay Lorsch have long explored the continuing struggle of organizations to achieve appropriate integration and differentiation. "Integration" refers to the need to link and coordinate the efforts and smooth the communications between organizational units. Most organizations at one time or another, find that many of their operating problems are rooted in a lack of coordination of efforts between units or departments–that the walls between units are just too high. Individual units may be doing just fine, but overall organizational effectiveness is suffering from a lack of sufficient integration.

On the other hand, some organizations discover that their effectiveness is suffering because their organizational units are not "differentiated" enough to deal with the variety of market challenges or customer demands that are being encountered. Perhaps a sales department needs to be partitioned to better know and service the needs of various market segments, or an engineering department oriented at applications engineering may now be insufficient to deal with emerging R & D needs–more differentiation is needed.

Initially, it may seem that these two variables lie on a single scale and become a matter of "either/or"–more of one results in less of the other. But organizations actually need both, and often in considerable amounts. The more diversity and uncertainty that an organization faces in its environment (customers, regulators, suppliers, etc.), the more differentiated its various organizational units must be to accommodate this diversity. But an organization must, at the same time, achieve sufficient integration among its various internal units to assure a smooth and coordinated overall effort. Both differentiation *and* integration require continued appraisal for sufficiency.

For internal service organizations it may be tempting to have an informal (and even unrecognized) internal goal of striving for ever-increasing differentiation. This distinguishes the internal service unit from all others, adds stronger internal control mechanisms, and reinforces a narrower identity–all desirable from the perspective of the individual unit. But this ignores the need for enhanced mechanisms that promote better integration of the unit with its environment (particularly its customers). An effective internal service unit needs to rise above the temptations of a narrow internal focus and build needed integration.

SOURCE: Paul R. Lawrence and Jay W. Lorsch, *Developing Organizations: Diagnosis and Action*, Reading, Mass.: (Addison-Wesley, 1969). For an updated version of this quest, see Dorothy Leonard-Barton, et.al., "How to Integrate Work *and* Deepen Expertise," *Harvard Business Review* (Sept./Oct. 1994), pp. 121-130.

mental and underlying assumptions about how and what gets done promotes a very open thought process at the beginning of action planning which ensures that no artificial ceilings on improvement levels are inadvertently built into the process.

Building Service Standards

Conflict around troubled internal service units often is rooted in vagueness and ambiguity of service delivery standards. What service is expected? Precisely how is it to be delivered? What roles are required? How is the service to be measured? Service standards may be ineffective for many reasons. In some cases no service standards exist at all. In others, there are too many standards or standards that are too general to be effective. In still other situations, service standards are poorly communicated or are not linked to appraisal and reward systems. Regardless of the cause, *if ambiguously defined service is delivered to satisfy unspecified service expectations and is not measured against any agreed-upon scale, confusion and conflict are the outcome.* Avoid this by articulating and negotiating specific service expectations and developing these into practical service standards.

An old adage notes that "performance doesn't improve unless you measure it," a maxim directly applicable to internal service turnaround efforts. Defining and measuring key quality-service variables is essential.

What is a Service Standard?

Service standards consist of two components: the *dimensions* of service performance that are important, and the *levels* of service that constitute "good service" in the minds of the customer. *Dimensions* are those standards the customer uses (implicitly or explicitly) to judge service. They could be timing, quality, quantity, cost, type, or location.

Define the smallest number of *dimensions* that encompasses the major customer needs. Federal Express, for example, began with a single performance standard—the dimension was "percentage of on-time deliveries" and the desired level was "100 percent on time." This standard was simple and effective in marketing efforts with external customers. For internal purposes, the single dimension was replaced with a set of twelve dimensions that described the various attributes of the service delivery process in much greater detail. The set included dimensions such as numbers of invoice adjustments, damaged packages, lost packages, and missed pickups—each with its own target level of service performance. This expansion of dimensions greatly improved Federal Express's ability to track, diagnose, and fix service problems promptly and to respond directly to customer evaluations of service quality.

Negotiating Standards

Customers of the internal service unit are very accessible (as compared to external customers) and usually eager to work on improved service. This is a great asset in developing explicit and agreed-upon service standards. The internal service unit must work with its customers to devise a list of service dimensions. Then, the two parties must agree on the *level* of acceptable service for each dimension. The *level* is the measure that characterizes acceptable service. Negotiating the *dimensions* and the *level* of service can be one of the most challenging, but most productive joint efforts for the customer unit and the supplier of internal service. The effectiveness of the future relationship is determined by the quality and acceptability of the conclusions reached in these deliberations.

Building a Customer Service Measurement System

Once you agree on a set of service standards, devise a method of measurability. Standards without practical means of tracking and reporting are nearly worthless. This measurement system needs to meet several criteria:

1. Both the customer unit and the service supplier must agree on precisely what service variables will be key to the service offering, and exactly what level of service within each of these variables will be deemed as good service.
2. The measurement data must be credible and must accurately represent actual performance. The data collection process, the data synthesis, and the reporting system should not be influenced by customers or service suppliers and must be viewed as having high integrity.
3. The service actually rendered will need to be measured regularly against the agreed-upon standards. Therefore, the measurement process must be practical, timely, and efficient.
4. The entire system should be set up to run almost automatically. Data should be gathered, processed, and reported on a regular basis by individuals who have this responsibility as a regular part of their ongoing duties.
5. The process must be rigid in that it cannot be changed frequently or revised at the whim of any party. It needs to be in-

sulated from accusations that poor showing in the results prompts pressure for revision in the measurement. There is a strong need for the development of an ongoing set of base service performance data—period-to-period comparability of data would be compromised by frequent changes to the system. It is possible that some initially agreed-upon variables just do not work as well as envisioned. In this case, a careful and studied revision is needed to make the system more effective or efficient. Hopefully, careful initial negotiation and planning minimizes the need for changes.

6. Develop quantitative measures whenever possible. The discipline helps clarify needs and provides more pointed feedback.

Revamping Internal Operations

The broad vision provided by a service strategy and the precision given by service standards equip the internal service unit with direction and definition. The challenge now is to channel this into internal processes and actions.

Begin the process with a clean slate. Remember you want to revamp internal processes and procedures so that they are aligned with newly defined customer needs and expectations. It can be tempting to retain old assumptions and procedures without serious challenge. Daniel Boorstin, the Librarian of Congress, Emeritus, in reflecting upon the process of the discovery of new insights, observed: "The greatest obstacle to discovering the shape of the earth, the continents, and the ocean, was not ignorance but the illusion of know ledge." In internal service organizations, fundamental, unchallenged assumptions may be the source of the service problems. Every organization has pragmatic constraints, but in order for you to revamp procedures, you must free yourself from the status quo. Ask the questions: What would happen if we just stopped performing this function? Or, how much does this really contribute to customer value added?

Organizational Waste

William Conway, a noted quality expert, suggests focusing on the discovery and elimination of organizational waste. Traditionally, *waste* is seen simply as the scrap or overage in a production process. But Conway defines waste broadly as all of the organizational time and resources that are expended in doing the wrong thing, not doing things correctly (the first time), reworking poorly done tasks, and inappropriate or ineffective coordination and interaction within an organization. Assess your internal service unit by asking: "If the ultimate customer could know and understand what I am doing in this action, would they be willing to pay for it?"

Waste can come in various modes:

- Mistakes and errors
- Breakdowns and delays
- Inefficiencies
- Variation in service quality

Waste can be thought of as the difference between what is actually happening in the organization and what could happen if all human and production systems were working as they should. Most executives would estimate present waste in their organizations at between 5 and 10 percent. A more realistic range is 20 to 40 percent. Executives who assume that present waste is 5 percent have low motivation to action. But those who realize that waste is actually closer to one-third of all actions have a different motivation.

The Cost of Quality

Assessing the *cost of quality* within an organization provides valuable internal process insights. The cost of quality is the sum of all resources expended in preventing errors, inspecting for errors, fixing errors before they reach the customer, and dealing with the consequences of errors that do reach the customer. In service companies these costs of quality are often greater than 33 percent of revenues.[1] Each additional dollar invested in prevention of failures could save up to ten dollars that is currently lost to internal failures (those that never reach the customer) and up to one hundred dollars lost to external failures (those that the customer sees). Investments in early elimination of waste generate substantial payoffs in performance and increased ability to meet the negotiated service standards.

Task and Process Restructuring

In the first three quarters of the twentieth century, a clear structure for ensuring quality in products or services evolved within business. Some individuals produced goods or services (production workers), and others inspected for defects and rejected inappropriate output (quality control inspectors or supervisors). The worker who produced the good or service felt little personal responsibility for its ultimate quality because that responsibility rested with the inspector. For manufacturers, the physical product could be scrutinized and the processes (or people) changed if quality moved too far out of desired bounds. For service businesses, the control process was much more problematic. Most services by their nature are ephemeral and expire immediately upon delivery. They cannot be easily examined after they've been delivered to determine whether or not they met some desired quality level. Because of this difficulty of monitoring, the need to have workers who are internally motivated to produce quality outcomes is much greater in service organizations.

Creating this intrinsic motivation and a sense of personal responsibility begins with overall restructuring of the work processes. Understanding and challenging the details of the present work flow and creatively reconfiguring them can yield work processes that are both efficient for the business and motivational for the workers.

Service Problem Identification and Recovery

Effectiveness in the revamped internal systems relies on the development of processes to provide quick *identification and handling of service problems*. Federal Express, for example, realized that data about service problems provides the essential key to improvement in service processes. They, therefore, develop an internal service problem identification system which they have dubbed the service quality index (SQI).

> "Rather than use success or failure rates, SQI takes a dozen different service failure events, counts them daily through Federal Express's far-flung operations, weights each according to the aggravation it causes customers. Fred Smith, the company's founder, calls them a 'hierarchy of horrors' and then totes up a day-by-day "goof score," the lower the better. A missed pickup or a lost package gets a weight of 10; a missing 'proof of delivery' is assigned a weight of 1. A dozen quality action teams, most headed by a vice president, work to locate spots where SQI hits bunkers and sand traps and then eliminate them. The company's management bonus is based on achieving SQI goals."[2]

Know When to Stop

The quality message has been received with much zeal in many organizations. However, in some it may go to uneconomic extremes. Frank R. McCullough, Senior Manager of Sales for Federal Express Corporation has noted a billboard near his home that reads "QUALITY ABOVE ALL." If this is the real practice of the company doing the advertising, one might want to sell their stock short. McCullough points out that any organization must find the point at which additional quality expenditure does not yield appreciable benefit to customers. Finding this point of diminishing returns in quality investment is what he terms "Quality Value Analysis." QVA is a tool to identify the factors that provide customer value in a product or a service, and then to determine the point of diminishing value in quality improvement on each of those factors. Once an organization has reached a point of diminishing returns for the customer on the improvement of a particular factor, customer value can best be enhanced by moving incremental resources and efforts to value improvement on other dimensions.

Motorola Corporation used a similar analysis to launch their now-famous "six sigma" quality program. They determined that the product quality target in their business needed to be at the level of only three defects per million units produced–at a level which is six standard deviations out (thus, "six sigma"). For Motorola this has resulted in $500 million annual savings. However, not every process or product needs to be at the "six sigma" level. Some examples of defect levels that actually occur:

TASK	NUMBER OF DEFECTS PER MILLION UNITS
IRS tax advice via phone	200,000
Doctor prescription writing	10,000
Average company	9,000
Airline baggage handling	8,000
Digital Equipment Company	900
Motorola, Inc. (actual)	90
Six sigma (best in class)	3
Domestic airline fatality rate	.7

Obviously, the domestic airlines do, and should, pursue an "error rate" that is quite different than that which is an appropriate investment for the IRS (even though the IRS could probably benefit from substantial quality improvement over the current state).

Sources: Frank R. McCollough, "Improved Customer Satisfaction Through Q.V.A.," *American Productivity & Quality Center Letter*, 10, (February 1991): 2; and Glenn Rifkin, "Pursuing Zero Defects Under the Six Sygma Banner," *New York Times* (January 13, 1991), 9F.

In this problem identification system, Federal Express uses readily collectible data and applies quantification that directly focuses on the problem areas. This results in a set of measures that is used effectively by work teams to attack a particular problem, or by senior management to monitor the overall health of the service systems.

Early service problem detection dramatically increases chances for good recovery. The goal of good problem identification systems is to find and fix a problem before the customer knows that one exists. A curious service irony is that many companies that are particularly good at avoiding problems (through excellent initial service delivery) may not have developed good recovery systems and expertise since they are not frequently needed. But most companies with numerous ongoing initial service problems also seem to have little competence in recovery.

Recovery, or how a service problem is handled, is a primary determinant of a continued positive customer relationship. If customer statements of concern about service are treated as points to be countered or debated, the stage is set for a confrontational interchange. If, however, the negative feedback is seen as an *opportunity for improvement*, the impact is reversed. This aggressive hunger for feedback from customers is the hallmark of an internal service organization moving toward excellence. Viewing complaints from customers or criticisms of internal systems as votes of no-confidence, or as "demerits" for the operators of the work system in question, may have been the historical mode. But engineering an internal transformation in which negative feedback is highly valued provides the lifeblood of improvement efforts. Such a transformation requires a strong about-face in the way these points of data are used in judging and rewarding individuals. In most existing systems everyone wants problems to be owned by someone else because of the guilt and recrimination associated with problem ownership. But this attitude must be turned around to encourage data flow about problems—the information which is required for improvement. Correcting problems is the valued behavior—denying or not correcting problems is the improper behavior.

When a service problem has occurred and the customer is contacted promptly by a service agent who is genuinely concerned with remedying the situation, what happens? The customer is eager to share data—data that only he or she has and that the service entity desperately needs. Information channels open, data flows, and the problem gets fixed. The service agent, in turn, reviews the data internally and revises systems to ensure that these types of problems do not occur again. Trust and respect grow between customer and service supplier. The basis for a service partnership is solidified.

Putting Chapter Twelve Ideas to Work

Here are questions to help promote thinking about how this material relates to your organization.

✓ What has been your organizations experience and success in setting and using service standards? What factors may have undercut these efforts?

✓ How would you go about analyzing and refining the entire service offering to eliminate unnecessary complexity and ensure low cost and high quality? What would the biggest challenges be in this effort?

✓ What might the key elements of a good service recovery system be in your particular internal service unit? What potential changes might smooth the functioning of this process?

Chapter 13

Linking the Plan to Others

Effective change plans require some key links to others outside the internal service unit. For many internal service units the historical weakness of these links has contributed strongly to the current problems. Fortunately, you have several avenues for directly strengthening these crucial links.

Building in "Boundary Spanners"

A troubled internal service unit tends to close its boundaries to insulate itself from the pain of negative feedback. This is particularly true if attempts to be receptive have failed. Often, the cultures of troubled internal service units place low emphasis on dealing effectively with outsiders. Therefore, few interface skills or capabilities have been fully developed.

The resulting barrier impedes communication between the internal service unit and outsiders. In essence it cuts off the very data required to improve and maintain excellent service. Specific mechanisms to break down the barrier and facilitate the flow of information to and from other parts of the organization are needed. These include the following:

- Regularly verify the expectations of key stakeholders.
- Provide open format meetings with customer representatives to discuss concerns and issues.
- Use benchmarking to see how other units are providing your kind of service in other organizations.
- Hold internal meetings that focus on the importance of data held by outsiders.

- Arrange "sabbaticals" in which selected internal service personnel serve with customer units on a temporary basis.
- Designate a full-time "boundary spanner" whose task is to analyze and improve the flow of crucial data across the departmental lines. (Rotate this job among selected departmental personnel every couple of months.)
- Analyze all internal processes and procedures from the perspective of the customer—determine the real *customer value-added* for each part of the process?

Building in these mechanisms promotes the full flow of undistorted data needed to provide excellent internal service.

Cost Allocation Systems

Most large organizations, particularly decentralized ones, have developed systems to allocate costs of internal service units to line functions. An effective cost allocation system manages and regulates central services in such a way that usage is based on real value received vs. cost. In these systems the total cost of internal service units (where no direct revenue is produced) is allocated to line units that add this cost to their own costs and apply them against their revenues to obtain a "bottom line." Theoretically this enables the line unit to evaluate itself like a stand-alone business and creates entrepreneurial incentives to keep costs in line and to maximize profit. But in practice, the method of allocating these overhead costs is often misunderstood or is judged as unfair and much of the motivational objective is defeated.

Most cost charge-backs come under considerable fire from managers. Although the real concern may be the line manager's feeling of vulnerability to internal service unit costs that he does not control, the objection is likely to be either that the overall service unit costs are too high or that the allocation mechanism is unfair. If overall internal service costs are seen as too high, the line manager may try to get more and more detailed cost data on the unit and then "help" the unit with suggestions on how it should manage its internal function better. This invasive action prompts conflict in a relationship that may have already been troubled.

Acceptance of a charge-back system hinges on perceived fairness. Perceived fairness is not only influenced by the specific attributes of the charge-back system itself, but also by the trust in the server/customer relationship.

A properly designed cost allocation system supports and guides the *alignment* of organizational elements with the overall goals of the change process itself. The system can help modify behavior within the organization in ways that better allocate scarce and expensive resources, and can serve as a monitor on the overall level of resources used by internal service units.

Charge-back systems should provide for:

1. *Understandability.* The link between charges and related activity should be clear to managers.
2. *Controllability.* Managers should be able to see how their actions and resource utilization decisions can control their charges.
3. *Cost/benefit incidence.* The charges should accrue to the operations that receive the benefit of the services being charged.
4. *Accountability.* A manager's performance evaluation should reflect effectiveness in internal resource utilization.[1]

Internal Performance Guarantees

Domino's Pizza built an empire on a simple service guarantee—your pizza in thirty minutes or three dollars off the bill. It was their performance guarantee. Innovative internal service units are offering similar performance guarantees as a way to back up their intent of excellent service. Offering a service guarantee is a bold action not to be taken without thoughtful consideration, but it can be a powerful vehicle for focusing and confirming excellence. A carefully planned internal service guarantee can:

1. focus the service unit on the explicit desired performance,
2. enhance service credibility with the customers, and
3. elicit useful feedback on performance areas that need improvement.

But to be effective from the customer's viewpoint the guarantee must be clear, directly related to the service, and easily collected. Internal performance guarantees are generally in the form of: "If [*level*] is not achieved with respect to [*dimension*], then the internal service unit will give [*dollars, time, benefit, or other specific compensation*]."

Internal Performance Guarantees

Here are some success stories from companies that implemented internal performance guarantees.

• *WESTINGHOUSE.* The Westinghouse Science and Technology Center (STC) had difficulties with its internal customers regarding project budgets, schedules, etc., and instituted the following internal guarantee:

1. Customers are to be kept advised of the cost and progress of an R&D project so that they can decide whether or not to continue the project.
2. STC agrees not to exceed costs on a project without prior customer approval.
3. If a change in project design or execution is required because of a mistake or miscalculation by STC, STC will pay the difference. For example, if the original project design specifies a particular component and it doesn't work correctly, STC will absorb the cost of the new component.

Offering this guarantee forced STC to work more closely with their customers in articulating project expectations, resulting in greatly improved service performance.

• *GTE.* The Management Education and Training Department of GTE dealt with concerns about ongoing training needs with a guarantee to each employee:

1. Each employee will have a minimum of forty hours of formal training each year or they may take an equivalent amount of outside training at company expense.
2. We guarantee that you will be satisfied with any course delivered at the GTE Management Development Center, or we will refund your tuition and room and board.

This guarantee forced a healthy examination of courses, instructors, and the needs of internal customers.

• *MARRIOTT* - The Human Resources Department at the Marriott Bethesda Hotel adopted the following guarantee to deal with some key needs of its internal customers:

1. Job applicants will receive an interview with the appropriate department within thirty minutes of the initial screening interview. Applicants who must wait longer will be given a complimentary dinner for two in the hotel restaurant.
2. HRD guarantees to find and refer qualified applicants to departments within two weeks of receiving a job requisition. If this guarantee is not met, the position will be filled with a temporary worker at the expense of the Human Resources Department.
3. Employees who find a payroll or benefit error on their paychecks will receive a complimentary dinner for two.

These guarantees have focused the HRD efforts, gained important performance feedback, and greatly improved internal service.

SOURCE: Christopher W.L. Hart, *Extraordinary Guarantees: A New Way to Build Quality Throughout Your Company and Ensure Satisfaction for Your Customers*, AMACOM, New York, 1993, pp. 108-114.

Proactive Communications

Information is the life-blood of the implementation of any change process. Without it, corrective adjustments to the process are impossible and the whole process goes off-track. Explicitly address the communications issue by focusing on two important factors. First, determine the ability to gather appropriate and timely data about the impact of actions. This information will be crucial to monitoring and tuning the change process. Secondly, analyze the direct flow of information to customers—much of their perception of service is shaped by the data provided by the service unit.

Benchmarking

Benchmarking is *the process of measuring one's products, services, and practices against the best organizations in order to produce changes in one's own organization.* The American Quality Foundation and Ernst & Young surveyed five hundred companies worldwide and found that 31 percent regularly benchmarked their products and services, and only 7 percent never did.

Internal service units have some advantages in gaining benchmarking information. Special groups with like technologies are formed by professional associations to share benchmarking information and techniques. In addition, internal service groups in other companies seem more willing to share ideas and performance data than their externally oriented line counterparts.

Benchmarking begins with a formal and detailed look at one's own internal processes and procedures. This breaks actions into discrete elements, each with its own key variables and measures. Internal service units can use benchmarking to look at:

- processes for framing and negotiating service standards
- specific service standard dimensions and levels employed
- internal service production processes
- mechanisms for relating to key stakeholders
- ways of gaining and utilizing customer unit feedback
- methods of achieving a customer-awareness focus
- service problem identification and recovery systems
- systems to identify and track customer service needs

External models that deliver excellence in an identified area of internal service must be identified. Look at direct competitors (Xerox

How to Get Started in Benchmarking

A benchmarking program can be launched through the use of a variety of resources.

Other Companies

Winners of the Malcolm Baldrige Quality Award are required to provide quality-related information and perspective to other interested firms. This has resulted in an unprecedented sharing of information about processes and systems that produce quality outcomes. Linda Crosby DeBerry, managing director of human resources at Federal Express, receives up to twenty requests per month to be a benchmark partner. Others in one's own industry or locale may also be helpful (see Appendix B for the list of winners).

Consultants

Several consulting firms act as neutral and formal clearinghouses for benchmarking information among clients. Some consulting firms such as A. T. Kearney, Towers Perrin, and Andersen Consulting have benchmarking groups. Other consultants, such as Best Practices Benchmarking (Lexington, Mass.), Oxford Associates (Bethesda, Md.), Saratoga Institute (Saratoga, Ca.), and the Hackett Group (Cleveland, Oh.), offer specialized benchmarking services.

Clearinghouses

Some nonprofit clearinghouses that assemble and distribute benchmarking data to their members include:

- *International Benchmarking Clearinghouse*—A benchmarking branch of the American Productivity & Quality Center in Houston - benchmarking training, white papers, networking personnel lists, and database information. Membership prices vary and confidential database information is only available to members. (713)685-4666.

- *Benchmarking Competency Center*—A service of the American Society for Quality Control (Milwaukee, Wis.)—provides benchmarking resources at low cost to interested parties. (414)272-8575.

- *Council on Benchmarking* - An offshoot of the Strategic Planning Institute in Cambridge, Mass.—is primarily a resource for member benchmarkers. (617)491-9200.

SOURCES: Barbara Ettorre, "Benchmarking: The Next Generation," *Management Review*, (June 1993), 10-16, and Jeremy Main, "How To Steal the Best Ideas Around," *Fortune*, (Oct. 19, 1992), pp. 102-106.

looked at Canon in the area of copiers, and DEC in workstations). Noncompetitors, too, can provide a valuable perspective (Xerox looked at the distribution function in L.L. Bean to determine how they performed so well, at GE for information systems, and at the Federal Reserve for bill-scanning processes).

This body of comparative data provides important stimulation and creativity as an internal service unit examines its own processes and procedures to determine a better route to excellence.

Causal Forces and Action Alternatives

As described in Part Two, a troubled internal service organization is plagued by debilitating forces. Throughout this chapter, action steps have been created which are necessary for an effective turnaround. Actions related to *creating a service strategy, building service standards, revamping internal operations,* and *linking the plan to others* will counter the effect of these forces. Your unit may have difficulty with particular forces. Other actions that address individual forces impacting internal service excellence are suggested.

Some Possible Specific Change Actions to Promote Internal Service Unit (ISU) Excellence

Possible Actions to Deal with the Apparent Monopoly

- Implement an internal billing system to focus on real costs.
- Conduct intensive session with ISU leadership focused on the nature and behavioral effects of the monopoly presumption.
- Benchmark comparable units on performance and costs units.
- Make outsourcing options more public and salient.
- Change ISU leadership.
- Re-examine formal and informal ISU vision, mission, goals, etc. and revise as needed to better align with service thrust.

Possible Actions to Deal with Internally Driven Culture

- Revise the recruiting/hiring criteria.
- Change rewards and recognition to focus on effectiveness and efficiency in service to other units.
- Make customer unit feedback a major part of ISU performance appraisal.

- Implement brief "internship" assignments in each other's work area for both ISU and their opposites in user areas.
- Facilitate permanent transfers between ISU and user areas.
- Educate ISU managers and staff on the overall business.
- Provide specific skills training for ISU managers and staff in consultation, customer service, handling irate customers, etc.
- Change ISU leadership.
- Collocate ISU staff with their primary users.
- Ensure ISU manager involvement in key organizational business activities and decisions.

Possible Actions to Deal with Misunderstandings over Expectations and Results

- Conduct study to detail current service issues/problems as seen by users, ISU staff, and ISU stakeholders.
- Hold session with ISU staff to review study findings and to prompt a need to change.
- Conduct training for ISU staff in the technology and importance of work outcomes measurement.
- Hold ISU staff session focused on the nature and importance of *a priori* explicitness and clarity of service expectations.
- Launch explorations with users to articulate specific service expectations, standards, and measurement systems.
- Educate all ISU staff and users on the agreed-upon service standards and measures—set appropriate expectations.

Possible Actions to Deal with Inefficient Service Offering

- Education ISU staff in the technology and methods of the quality movement regarding work analysis, measurement, and complexity.
- Benchmark ways others minimize complexity.
- Study existing work systems in detail to be able to launch appropriate internal work analysis of the present state.
- Conduct user and costing study to gather cost/value data on existing and potential service offerings.
- Restructure entire existing service offering set to reduce complexity and costs while raising reliability.
- Work with user group to gain acceptance of a less complex, but more efficient and reliable service offering set.

Putting Chapter Thirteen Ideas to Work

Here are questions to help promote thinking about how this material relates to your organization.

✓ How could your organization go about developing "boundary spanners" to strengthen communication and linkages between internal service units and their customer units?

✓ How much controversy exists in your organization about the cost allocation system and internal service units? What potential changes might smooth the functioning of this process?

✓ What types of internal service guarantees might be offered by your unit? What would be the major problems associated with them?

✓ What sources of relevant performance benchmarking information exist for your unit? How could you obtain and utilize this data?

PART VI
IMPLEMENTATION
Using the plan to achieve service excellence

Introduction

The success of an internal service change plan is totally dependent upon the skills, attitudes, and behaviors of the people who must implement it. In the chapters of this part of the book three essential topics are addressed that must be mastered by any internal service unit driving to world class performance:

- Aligning the culture
- Developing "service people"
- Building in continuous improvement

Review our place on the process map below, then proceed to the conclusion of the Mid-Americorp case.

The Process Map
The Major Process Steps in Creating an Internal Service Performance Turnaround

1. *Assessment/Commitment*
   What is the overall nature and scope of this change—is this change what we want to do?

2. *Information Gathering*
   What do we need to know to make this change successful?

3. *Action Planning*
   What specific changes need to be made?

4. *Implementation*
   How can people best put the planned changes into effect to create service excellence?

Chapter

CASE: Mid-Americorp —
Driving to World Class Performance

Bill Walker, head of the Information Systems Division of Mid-Americorp, felt that the action plan to engineer a performance turnaround within his unit was essentially developed and ready for implementation. He decided to wait three months before kicking off the plan so that individuals affected could be prepared for the changes.

Walker knew that the supervisors within the division could make or break the plan as it was implemented. He planned a two-day training session for IS Division supervisors that focused on changing the supervisory role from its traditional emphasis on direction to one that stressed facilitation. This was a tough transition because the belief that "a good supervisor is a directive supervisor" had been reinforced for years. But as the group explored the benefits of moving to a more empowered work force and the related necessary changes in supervisory behavior, the need to change style became more clear.

Creation of the "CIP" Teams

With the supervisory group preparing for their new roles, Walker's attention now moved to the employees. Each employee was grouped with a small number of colleagues in a natural work team—each team was called a Continuous Improvement Project (CIP) team. This organization promoted additional interaction and deliberation to support the improvement effort. Meetings were held each week throughout the initial month with CIP teams focusing on the new operating environment. In these initial meetings, an external facilitator and the supervisor set out the task and helped the team get itself organized relative to the upcoming changes. In subsequent meetings, the supervisor moved to a more facilitative role and the leadership of the team began to evolve from within the team itself. This was another tough transition, but most CIP teams had taken energetic command of their work sessions by the end of the second week. Additional training in customer interface management was conducted for those IS employees who had direct contact with customer units.

The Chargeback Issue

During the last month before implementation, Jonathan Greyson, the CEO of Mid-Americorp, had received a barrage of inquiries from managers of divisions that were customers of Information Systems regarding what their costs (in the internal costing system) would be after the changes. He thought that the issue had been dealt with in the planning efforts but the concern was still very strong. Within Mid-Americorp, managers of line divisions were charged directly with a rather arbitrary share of the corporate "overhead" generated from staff divisions like IS. The amount of these charges directly affected the reported bottom-line performance for these divisions and, therefore, was a matter of deep concern. Greyson met with Walker and the heads of the customer divisions to review charge-back concerns.

The line managers wanted a charge-back system that provided a fair charge based on actual usage; was clear and understandable; allowed line managers substantial control over charges through modification of their consumption of services; and was based on actual IS costs which would be carefully monitored for reasonableness and tested against potential outside suppliers.

Walker agreed with these desired characteristics, but also wanted a system that prohibited purchase of outside IS services for a two-year period (after that, limited purchase would be possible but this would allow time to get IS services and costs in line); and encouraged IS service utilization by line divisions that reflected real IS costs for each service (some services were now priced artificially low encouraging over-usage and distortion of scarce IS resources). The accounting group developed a charge-back system that met these objectives.

Program Launch

Kickoff day came and went with few problems. Early feedback on the change process was very encouraging. The CIP teams felt a mixture of anxiety and eagerness as they began the process of measuring performance against the standards that had previously been agreed upon. They obtained current performance feedback, performed analysis, and made needed system changes. The team would be first to review performance feedback. Only later would this information go to top management for monitoring—this allows the CIP teams to measure, monitor, and correct their own processes of service delivery.

The more intense interactions with customer units over the last few months had promoted a more positive feeling among the IS division and its customers. Walker could see a new attitude about customers emerging within the division and could sense the positive effect that this was having with customers. Improvements were more than perceptual. The substantial operational and procedural changes had added new service power and efficiency. Initial protests from customers about a narrowed range of services died quickly as customers experienced noticeably higher levels of service quality and responsiveness on the services that they received.

Adjustment and Tuning

Walker realized that it would be easy to let down after the initial successes. Sixty days after the program launch he personally visited each customer unit and interviewed unit representatives about their perception of the service that they were receiving. He solicited suggestions for improving the process which he passed along to the relevant CIP teams for action. He formulated his information into a summary progress report for Greyson and key customer unit managers.

In addition, Walker set up a regular schedule of "customer insight visits" in which individual IS personnel would spend a day working with their primary customer counterpart. These visits greatly enhanced understanding of the kind of problems and issues that the customers faced in their tasks. The program went so well that two primary customer groups asked to set up a reverse program that would allow their people to spend time within IS to see that side of the operation—a request which Walker was delighted to grant.

Within a couple months the CIP teams had really become the "custodians" of quality. They were directly gathering information, performing analysis, and making needed changes in the systems and processes. Empowerment was working and bureaucracy and overhead declined.

A few supervisors continued to have real difficulty with the transition in role. They felt that their historical role had been one of importance—importance generated by a position in which all information flowed to them for decisions and action. Now, much of this function was held directly by the CIP teams. For some this was not a comfortable role. Walker worked with these individuals and had success in helping two of them adapt to the new role. However, in four other cases, repeated efforts met with no success. Two of these individuals elected to retire and the other two transferred into other divisions with traditional supervisory roles. None were replaced, since the need for a large number of first-line supervisors had significantly diminished as the CIP teams took on more and more responsibility.

The First Year's Results

At the one-year anniversary of change implementation, the performance results of the division, as measured by the service standards which had been agreed upon fifteen months earlier, were compiled. The ten objective measures had been combined into an overall "quantitative service index" that measured the distance between actual performance and the quantitative service standards. A second index summarized the six qualitative evaluation factors into a "subjective service index." The senior managers of the IS Division tracked these two aggregate indices to provide a quick check on overall progress and used the more detailed individual indices to begin diagnosis of any specific emerging problems with the CIP teams. The gratifying picture that had emerged after a full year of operation is presented on the next page.

IS PERFORMANCE
First Year of New Program Operation

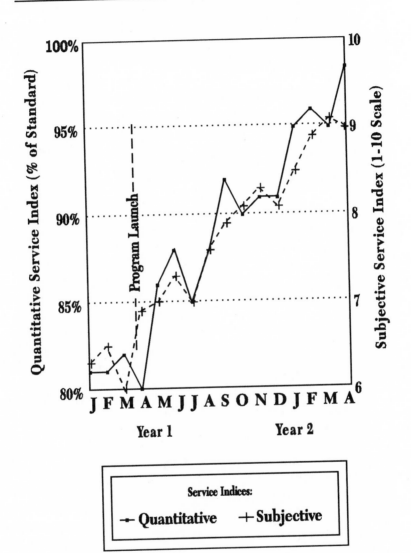

Other IS division changes were beginning to pay off. While cost charge-backs continued to be a concern for the line managers, they were now focused on exploring the reason for specific charges or ways to reduce utilization—exactly what was intended. The measures and standards of service were working well, too. Some minor revisions were negotiated for easier measurement or more focus, but they had essentially remained in place as designed. These standards had clarified service expectations and provided specific appropriate measures of service rendered.

Greyson was particularly gratified when the head of Mid-Americorp's marketing department approached him about constructing a new marketing campaign for the company that would center on a "service guarantee" to the external customers of Mid-Americorp regarding perfect bank statements and account handling. This would place the IS Division in a highly visible position. Greyson saw it as just what was needed to solidify the positive performance results of the department. A program was developed that offered external customers ten dollars for any error in a statement or banking transaction. An advertising campaign was launched publicizing the offer and emphasizing the excellence in service quality offered by Mid-Americorp. The campaign was a remarkable success. At the time, the two main competitors of Mid-Americorp were having significant quality and performance problems in their internal IS units and Mid-Americorp benefited strongly from the contrast. During the three-month campaign, Mid-Americorp had to pay for fewer than two hundred errors out of 200 million items handled (most of these were encoding errors that had been committed by other banks, but were paid anyway). This success helped raise pride within the IS unit and solidified its new performance position with other Mid-Americorp units. Seeing the IS Division as a source of external competitive advantage was a new, but welcomed, experience for Mid-Americorp.

The most telling incident of the change process occurred about two years after the change plan was implemented. The firm that had proposed providing contract IS services to Mid-Americorp made another presentation to Jonathan Greyson and four key board members. Once again, they promised significant cost savings for Mid-Americorp and high levels of service if the present internal IS Division was converted to an external contract operation run by the outside company. Greyson discussed the proposal with various bank presidents and was immediately met with cries of protest. The sentiment was best expressed by the head of the largest bank: "We had terrible IS service and now have worked our way into terrific service. I, for one, have no desire to give up responsive, effective, and cost-sensitive IS services for some external company that makes promises." The other presidents echoed similar support for IS and the proposal was dropped. It was clear to Greyson that the change process had been a great success.

Putting Chapter Fourteen Ideas to Work

Here are questions to help promote thinking on how this material relates to your organization.

✓ How experienced is your organization in utilizing work teams, such as the Mid-America "CIP" teams? How much experience have you had in fully empowering work teams?

✓ How could you best prepare your organization to be effective in handling unexpected issues during implementation of a change plan?

✓ How could you use the Mid-Americorp model to help your internal service organization press on to even greater achievement after it has accomplished the initial goals?

The Culture of Internal Service Excellence

Aligning the Culture

Every interacting work group—a jury, a military squad, a sports team, or an internal service unit—develops informal guidelines and values that shape member views and behaviors. This shared *organizational culture* helps individuals understand the functioning of the unit and their role and expected behavior within it. It also influences the service delivery interactions and performance of the entire unit.

Troubled internal service units often have a culture that is *internally driven*, a negative force contributing to internal service performance problems (see Chapter Five). Employees focus on their own department, their own technology, their own needs, and their own values. This inward focus so dominates the viewpoints and behavior of individual service unit people that they tend to ignore the needs of the customers they are serving. This can destroy efforts at service excellence. Therefore management must aggressively replace that culture with one that is strongly aligned with the new direction of the emerging internal service unit.

The Role of Culture

Culture can be evaluated on both *strength* and *fit*. A strong culture has many elements that are mutually reinforcing and can have great influence over individual behavior, while a weaker culture is less internally aligned and exhibits less influence over behavior. Some cultures *fit* particularly well as reinforcers of key desired values while others do not support positive accomplishment and have a poor fit.

For example, IBM worked for decades building and supporting a very strong sales-oriented organizational culture. It achieved strength and market share through aligning elements of personnel selection and promotion criteria, language, and dress code to reinforce the desired culture. Its culture strongly shaped employee behavior and was a real source of competitive advantage in the marketplace. But the strong culture that had created competitive advantage in an earlier time became a hindrance in adapting to the changing computer technology market of the late 1970s and early 1980s. The previously beneficial cultural characteristics inhibited creativity, entrepreneurship, and adaptability to the birth of a new computing technology known as microprocessing.

Early symptoms of IBM's cultural limitations appeared in 1976 when Steven Jobs and Steve Wozniak (then twenty-one and twenty-six years of age, respectively) introduced the Apple II Personal Computer. With a very large stake in the big mainframe computers of the day, IBM lined up to protect its market share from assault by the new computing interloper. The IBM culture promoted mainframe computing as "the computing solution." Although public interest in microcomputing mounted, IBM culture caused the company to ignore signs of market changes—the culture that was so successful in dealing with large mainframe systems was just not sufficiently agile and quick to respond to the challenges of a new computing market. Apple, and other "upstarts" were taking customers, growing market share, and romping through the new computer markets of opportunity.

IBM finally recognized the conflict between the traditional culture and current market needs. A special task force was established to quickly develop an IBM microcomputer market entry. This task force was physically and emotionally isolated from the main IBM cultures and its accompanying "rules." The group successfully used this cultural isolation and determined that timing and market demands required incorporating parts and software already developed by others into the new IBM product (a strong violation of traditional IBM values). The final outcome was the development of a solid PC product in record time. In 1981, IBM introduced its own microcomputer, producing sales of 800,000 units in 1982. Playing quick catch-up, IBM was on its way to becoming the industry standard in PCs. It succeeded largely because it recognized that a culture that was previously a source of great strength, can also become a competitive death shroud under swiftly changing market conditions. IBM had a strong culture, but one that didn't fit with a dynamic new technology environment. Realigning the fit between culture and market needs enabled IBM to regain competitiveness.

Exxon, too, has developed a strong and effective culture that supports its accomplishments. Individuals in this culture have learned to work and interact in ways that facilitate success in the mature, relatively steady business of finding, processing, and selling petroleum products. Exxon is excellent in applying technical analysis to fine-tune systems. But as internal capital accumulated in the 1970s, Exxon searched for diversification opportunities that would insulate the company from oil industry downturns, use available cash, and provide an outlet for their considerable managerial talent pool.

Exxon entered the rapidly growing office products market and established Exxon Office Product Systems to manufacture and market various types of office automation equipment. The new company utilized the main elements of the traditionally successful Exxon management culture. But as the company quickly learned, a culture that is very good at fine-tuning a long-term process may be much too inflexible to compete effectively in the rapidly shifting office products market. Fortunately, Exxon recognized the gross mismatch of culture and market requirements, and exited the venture.

So, is having a strong culture good or bad? The answer is an ambiguous "yes." The relationship is not simple. Harvard Business School professors John Kotter and James Heskett identified twenty-two strong culture companies and divided them into high and low performers, based upon actual corporate results.[1] Industry analysts who were familiar with the companies described the contribution culture had played in their performance. Eighty-three percent of the responses about the higher performing firms concluded that culture had helped performance. Interestingly, sixty percent of the responses about the lower performers concluded that culture had hurt performance. As in the cases of IBM and Exxon, a strong culture may work for or against performance—depending on whether or not the culture is strategically appropriate. It is strategically appropriate if the culture's values and norms provide a good *fit* with the competitive or strategic needs of the company. High-performing companies are much more likely to have cultures that place high value on excellent leadership, particularly leadership that shows concern for the key stakeholders (customers, stockholders, and employees).

For internal service units these are relevant lessons. Both *strength* and *fit* of culture are important and manageable. Now, let's look at some of the specific ways to develop an effective culture.

Values as a Cultural Element

Organizational culture has at its core a set of underlying *values* that are promoted and supported. Values specify what is prized in the organization, how one "gets ahead," what is taboo, and how one can stumble in career advancement. They provide guidance in choosing between alternative actions. The impact of cultural values on service excellence is closely related to how well *aligned* these basic values are with the ultimate goals of the organization.

The Walt Disney Company invests considerable time and effort to ensure that every element of its culture supports and reinforces its goal of trying to exceed the expectations of its guests. Personnel selection focuses on values of friendliness, personal initiative, and appearance to ensure that staff fit well into the Disney culture. Each staff member receives intensive training at Disney University to clarify expectations, and to cultivate the needed attitudes and skills. Each job and work group is surrounded by constant reminders of the Disney culture—that underlying set of values and behaviors that yield consistently excellent experiences, "one guest at a time." Disney ensures that all elements of the work experience support and reinforce the values that contribute to a positive Disney experience for the guest.

Aligned cultural values are strong forces, but may not reinforce the right goals. The central values in a troubled internal service unit may be the enhancement of an internal technology or alignment with a particular professional group. Unless the values center on *service to the customer*, the power generated through culture can dissipate in less productive directions.

Reinforcements as Cultural Elements

Once desired values are established, reinforce them and make them salient for members of the organization with appropriate language, designations of excellent individual performance, ceremony, and recognition. Elements for reinforcement include:

1. *Language.* The language used within the work group serves as a solid reminder of a mindset and approach. An internal service unit that serves "users" acts differently than one that has

Disney-Speak

The Disney organization is probably one of the most thorough in using everyday language to reinforce the cultural norms and expectations of the organization. In Disney theme parks, the primary goal of each employee is to ensure that each customer has their expectations exceeded. However, there are no employees and no customers! Employees are "cast members" at Disney and a customer is a "guest."

This is much more than semantics. It is an aggressive reinforcement of a cultural mindset. Disney has concluded that its ultimate service goals can best be met if everyone has constant reminders that they are in "show business." All language reflects this idea.

For example, cast members don't wear uniforms, they wear costumes. They are either onstage or backstage. The human resources department is referred to as "central casting." All support devices are props. Every element of the language helps to provide constant reminders to each cast member that he or she is there to ensure a quality experience for the guest–the desired cultural value.

SOURCE: Dennis A. Snow, "Management: Disney Style," management seminar at Lake Buena Vista, Fla., Feb. 25, 1994.

"customers." A "user" simply uses your services—not a very demanding role for the supplier. But a "customer" has needs that must be actively explored and met to their satisfaction— quite a different, and much more challenging task. Many organizations carefully and consciously decide whether they are serving "customers," "users," "patients," "clients," "guests," "buyers," "patrons," "consumers," or "callers." These may sound like a set of synonyms defining the same group of individuals, but careful selection of terminology influences the attitude service providers develop toward these individuals. The specific words used for other parts of the work process also can be cultural reinforcements. Service people who see themselves as "employees" behave differently than "associates" or "consultants." Are service agents "helping clients solve their problems" or "handling complaints?" Obviously, simply changing language alone is not sufficient to change behavior significantly. But words and language can be important reinforcements of a broader cultural value.

2. *Heroes.* Heroes who personify desirable values of the culture are another important element of reinforcement. Original company founders (e.g., Henry Ford, Tom Watson, John D. Rockefeller, and Steven Jobs) can serve as a company hero and

The Making of a Hero

An internal service unit, a company, or even an entire country needs a culture which reinforces characteristics and behaviors which are particularly helpful to the achievement of it's goals. Heroes of the culture can characterize the desired values and behaviors in ways that may be more effective than almost any other means. The organization can assist this process by spotlighting and reinforcing existing heroes that personify the desired values, However, in some cases it can be very useful to create a hero.

On April 18, 1942, Jimmy Doolittle made history by launching sixteen B-25 bombers from the carrier Hornet to bomb Tokyo. But despite the bravery of his deed, Doolittle was severely depressed. He had inflicted only minor damage on Tokyo, had lost all sixteen airplanes, and many of the aircrews. In early 1942, however, the United States desperately needed a hero that personified courage and determination. President Roosevelt decided that Doolittle was going to be it. By the time Doolittle returned to the United States, such a "hero-creating" process had occurred that he was surely the only person in the U.S. who did not feel that he deserved his Medal of Honor. Thus, Jimmy Doolittle joined Rosie the Riveter and others to symbolize the values and behaviors that the United States needed so desperately in so many of its citizens in the coming months and years.

Organizational units, too, can use "heroes" to personify desired skills or performance. An internal service unit that rewards and spotlights individuals of high technical accomplishment is sending a very different signal to its members than one that reinforces excellence in identifying and meeting the needs of customer units.

a role model exemplifying the desired values. Recognition of heroes defines desired characteristics. Seeing a particular person who represents certain values is not only motivational, it also makes those desirable values more explicit and clear—"that is the standard, and I can do it too." The most visible characteristics of an organizational hero will shape the behavior of others. Is the hero a maverick or faithful plodder, hard worker or a friend to all, a creator or a tuner, a bold leader or a conservative risk avoider? The creation of an organizational hero provides a powerful channel for expressing the desired cultural values. Traditional internal service heroes may have been technical experts or successful crusaders for or defenders of the unit's interests against outsiders. Send a new message through consistent public rewards to and reinforcement of someone who is truly passionate about customer service or who successfully bridges departmental boundaries.

3. *Ceremony.* Use ceremony within the organization to reinforce the values of the culture. How meetings are conducted, how greetings are exchanged, how organizational victories are celebrated, and how information is transferred are important ceremonial elements in a culture. Ceremonies and rituals can be seen as superfluous wastes of time and energy, but they express and nurture the desired cultural values. These social and organizational rituals can determine how individuals relate to each other, as well as what is to be celebrated in the organization. Observe and understand the ritualistic value of existing practices within an organization before eliminating them or substituting others. These elements of culture, too, can be shaped into reinforcements of the desired cultural values.

4. *Reward systems.* Align the formal and informal reward system with the desired cultural values. Base formal performance appraisal systems, promotions, raises, as well as informal "atta-boys," or "atta-girls," on the same underlying values that are desired within the unit. Are people explicitly evaluated and rewarded on their effectiveness in determining and meeting customer unit needs, in dealing well with the customer, and in being a great boundary spanner? Too often, the real (or perceived) rewards vary from the stated values, creating a substantial and justified cynicism regarding the gap between what is said and what is really desired. Employees are unlikely to become more customer-oriented, if the major rewards and recognition continue to go to those representing values of technical excellence alone.

Service Culture vs. Professionalism

Most internal service units are lead or managed by professionals—accountants, computer specialists, lawyers, marketers, etc. They joined the service unit only after considerable professional training and socialization in the norms and values of a professional subculture. Professional societies and associations provide intellectual stimulation and network relationships for many individuals. These professional cultures reinforce values of expertise, specialization, technical knowledge, and independence of judgment. But values that ensure quality within the profession may be in direct conflict with the drive to serve customer needs.

Strong professional subcultures promote quality professional outcomes (often a strong asset) and support a belief that the professionals should function with considerable autonomy and act to maximize professional quality and technology. But an effective internal service unit asks the professional to place the customer at the top of the priority list. Most professional training lacks emphasis on serving customers. The result is a real conflict between these two micro-cultures. Serving a customer's needs may mean compromising a solution from a professional perspective. Or, creating the very best professional outcome may have little to do with serving the real needs of customers.

Marketing departments may strive to win "Addys" (a coveted national advertising award), an information systems department may strive to install and use the very latest computer systems (high status in the profession), and a human resources department may be eager to implement the latest training devices. But each of these efforts may miss important elements of servicing their internal customers whose needs may have little to do with the "best and latest" equipment or techniques. In each of these cases, the informal values of the *professional micro-culture* may directly conflict with the desired values of a *customer-centered micro-culture*. High standards of professionalism must be maintained. But the challenge in installing a customer-driven culture is to find ways to help the professional confront this conflict and resolve it with a priority on customer need satisfaction.

Culture Modification

Changing the powerful and complex force of organizational culture requires a detailed understanding of the specific nature and functioning of the current culture. Each current cultural element serves some positive function for individuals. You can't successfully replace an old cultural element without fully understanding the positive function that it serves. Many organizational change efforts lie dead or dormant because individuals resisted the displacement of cultural elements that had value to them.

Often, major elements of the existing culture can be incorporated into the new, avoiding the tougher task of outright displacement of major existing cultural values. A basic culture that is supportive of the values needed for change may require only minor strengthening or modification. In this case, focus the change plan on better articulation and reinforcement. If the existing culture supports values that are in conflict with the desired future direction of the internal service unit or, if the values are not internally consistent, plan on a major overhaul or replacement of the culture.

Develop a clear definition of the dominant characteristics of the present culture and of the desired culture. Identify qualities that are currently valued or rewarded and those that will be valued or rewarded in the new culture. This deliberation can aid the change team in understanding the contrast between where they've been and where they're going. An example of a specific statement of contrasting cultural elements might be:

What is Valued or Rewarded in Our Culture?

Present culture	*Desired culture*
- Build more power for the department	- Be skillful in gaining insights into the real needs of customer units
- Demonstrate superior technical prowess	- Be excellent in "going the extra mile" to meet customer needs
- Expand the department's domain or influence	- "Boundary-span" to link the department with others
- Fend off assaults on the department by "outsiders"	- Build effective systems to measure and modify service rendered

This type of articulation can be very helpful in directing the needed migration to the desired culture and in identifying possible blockages and resistances. It also describes the cultural change to individuals beyond the team (stakeholders, customers, other employees, etc.)

The concept of *organizational culture* forms the foundation on which organizations function and accomplish work. Take an active and skillful hand in modifying organizational culture so that it will emerge to genuinely and totally support performance goals. Culture starts at the top. A main difference between a manager and a leader

Safety vs. Macho - A Cultural Dilemma

Management consultant Charles Hampden-Turner reports on a major oil company that wished to change its safety performance–particularly for the drivers of gasoline tank trucks. The prior safety record was not acceptable and had to be improved.

Careful examination of the existing cultural values concerning safety identified a major conflict between the encouragement of safety goals and the self-image of the truckers. The drivers (members of the Teamsters Union) saw themselves as "knights of the road"–macho, self-reliant, tough, and individualistic. Historical admonitions by the company to "be safe" were seen as attempts at control and were in direct conflict with this self-image.

The company re-examined its approach to safety and changed to one that incorporated this self-image of individualism into the desired role. The drivers were engaged as paid consultants to help redesign vehicles, procedures, and even roads to improve safety. Much was done to create a new "culture of heroism" in which the drivers were seen as heroic crusaders for the cause of safety. Even the CB radios (which had been a primary tool for expression of individualism) became a tool for warning others of hazards or problems. These activities and actions were publicly recognized by the company.

The key to turning around the safety situation lay in recognizing the elements of the existing culture and designing a new culture that incorporated and used these elements rather than tried to extinguish them.

SOURCE: Charles Hampden-Turner, *Creating Corporate Culture: From Discord to Harmony*, Reading, MA: Addison-Wesley, 1992, pp. 64-77.

is the ability to successfully understand, realign, and build organizational culture as a powerful force for creating and reinforcing excellent performance.

Putting Chapter Fifteen Ideas to Work

Here are questions to help promote thinking about how this material relates to your organization.

✓ What are the *dominant drivers* (themes or goals) of the present culture in your internal service unit? How do you see these influencing everyday service from the unit?

✓ How *strong* is the culture in your present internal service unit? What are the major reinforcing elements that keep this culture strong?

✓ How *aligned* is the culture with the needed levels of service and cost? Do the members of the unit feel a sense of misalignment?

16
Chapter

Development of "Service People"

The quality of individual service interactions depends heavily on the service motivation and interpersonal skills of the people executing them. We have all experienced service personnel who have non-service attitudes or low interpersonal skills. But we have also had the joy of dealing with real "service people." They tune into our needs, treat us with respect, and handle our service transaction with knowledge and skill. We go back to them as often as possible. The differences between the two is more than just style or personality. Internal service excellence requires determining exactly what makes a "service person" and how to develop one.

Respect and Skill at the "Moments of Truth"

In the information-gathering stage, the customer's "moments of truth" were identified and analyzed (See Chapter Ten). These moments of truth are the defining interactions between customer and service supplier that shape the customer's evaluation of service. The moments of truth usually involve direct personal contact between a service agent and the customer. The treatment the customer receives during those moments heavily influences overall judgments of not only the specific service rendered, but also of the entire service organization.

Ensuring consistent high quality for the customer in each moment of truth is a paramount objective for the effective internal service unit. The quality of that moment of truth is heavily determined by the attitude of the server. A recent Gallup survey asked over one thousand consumers to define the elements of "quality service." The most frequently mentioned items were aspects of direct human contact—courtesy, positive attitude, and helpfulness.

For the individual server, willingness and ability to use interpersonal skills are vital. Although the particular tasks involved in each job vary, some of the specific interpersonal and problem-solving skills that are required of internal service unit customer contact personnel are listed on the next page.

Individuals vary immensely in their predisposition and experience in these skills—aggressive screening is required to find the naturals. Then, train contact personnel thoroughly to ensure a service attitude and the necessary set of skills to effectively handle the moments of truth.

The issues of interpersonal power and contact overload further affect the server/customer interaction and need to be explored. Contact with the customer shapes the server/customer relationship. If the service supplier acts in ways that demonstrate power over the customer during the moment of truth transaction, the human quality of the interaction deteriorates for the customer. But if the service supplier shows respect for the customer, perceived quality goes up. This is particularly important for internal service organizations because of the temptation for the server to make explicit the "captive user" aspect of the relationship (a behavioral side effect of the assumption that the service unit has an apparent monopoly position). This behavior emphasizes the lack of customer power and control in the situation and makes customers feel a need to balance the power situation by exercising whatever power they feel they might have over the service supplier (evaluation, coalitions with others, etc.). Remove power-oriented trappings from these interactions to enhance the individual moments of truth and the subsequent evaluations of service quality.

Contact overload creates severe stress for personnel who are constantly facing customers. Ceaseless customer contact requires continuous attention to the needs and emotional state of the customer. This can be exacerbated by a service supplier's tendency to feel personal responsibility for the customer's problems. Effectively managing this stress requires a high degree of maturity, a positive self image, and supportive coping mechanisms. In well-run service situations like Disney's theme parks, employees go "offstage" to "get out of character"—temporarily removing themselves from the intense personal performance pressure. Other high-pressure service businesses such as hospitals, airlines, and sales organizations have established employee support groups to help address this contact overload pressure.

Required Customer Contact Skills

ISU/Customer Interface Task	*Required Skills of ISU Contact Person*
Help customer unit identify and define service needs	- Active listening - Problem analysis - Trust-building - Data-gathering - Partnership-building communications style
Receive and fill customer unit service request	- Active listening - Confirming and clarifying - Does not express dominance or power - Inspires confidence in technical competence
Handle service breakdowns and recovery	- Deal with emotionally charged (hostile) people - Respond to feelings, not just content of communications - Accept responsibility to fix problem (no denial) - Non-threatening communications style
Communicate service status and reporting	- Clearly organized communications - Non-defensive responses - Inspire confidence in technical competence - Seek additional feedback - Enlist acceptance and confirmation

Empowerment

Successful use of the people in an internal service unit requires that the optimum placement of decision-making responsibility and power be carefully determined. Information must flow to this location and control is vested there. In more traditional organizations, decision-making and control resides with the top manager. In more decentralized units, much of this power and control has been moved to the middle managers and supervisors. Now, many units are benefiting from moving decision-making even further down in the organization — to teams of workers. Some decision-making and responsibility will be at every level in the organization but deciding on the optimum level of empowerment requires that the location of the concentration of decision-making be identified.

While empowerment of workers has prompted some dramatic productivity successes, it has not been without problems. No single answer is right for every internal service unit, but most could improve effectiveness by moving further toward empowerment of workers. Let's look at the change factors that might encourage such migration within an internal service unit:

- *External customer satisfaction* is closely related to internal employee satisfaction about the way that they, themselves, are managed.
- *Employee satisfaction* is strongly related to self perceptions of the importance of their work.
- The sense of *significance and contribution* in work can best be enhanced by providing real decision-making and authority to the individuals actually doing the service task.

Since personal attitude and intrinsic motivation is so crucial in a service moment of truth, the potential gain from this change can be very significant.

Employees require four things to be successfully empowered:

- *Knowledge and understanding* to contribute to service unit improvements
- *Information and feedback* about their service unit processes and performance
- *Authority and power* to make and implement decisions that influence service unit direction and performance
- *Rewards and recognition* based on their service unit performance

Giving employees these four components within a supporting change program equips them to contribute to the internal service unit at a much higher level. But empowering employees involves a series of tradeoffs that need to be carefully considered. Some of these are:

Empowerment Tradeoffs

Benefits of Empowerment	*Costs/Risks of Empowerment*
- Improved response time to customer's service delivery needs	- Increased investment in personnel selection and training
- Improved response time to recover from service problems	- Increased labor costs
- Improved employee job satisfaction and feeling of self worth	- Startup difficulties in the transition period
- Enhanced warmth and enthusiasm in customer interactions	- Adjustment difficulties as supervisors move from direction to facilitation
- Increased opportunities for employees to directly improve service	- Key commitments of unit resources made by people with less perspective and scope of vision

Nordstrom Department Stores are renowned for their extreme position on employee empowerment. Nordstrom expects employees to take a great deal of personal initiative in discovering and meeting customer needs. This approach has earned them a remarkable, almost legendary, reputation with this policy, among other service firms and their customers. In fact, the Nordstrom company policy manual is one sentence long: "Use your own best judgment at all times." But this extreme level of empowerment is not right for all. Some cautious managers cite the story of the Four Seasons Hotel doorman that left work and took a flight to return a briefcase left behind by a guest— empowerment may require some bounds.

Empowerment can be an energizing source of new improved performance and positive service effectiveness for an internal service unit. How much and whom to empower are decisions that need to be carefully weighed.

Supervisory Roles

Few things can sink a change effort faster than a supervisory group that does not understand the change, does not support the change, or does not have the skill to facilitate it. Because of a supervisor's key leadership position, he or she is on the cutting edge of implementation effectiveness. Supervisors represent management and the company to most workers and they must be assertive and effective facilitators of the change process.

If supervisors have been involved in the key deliberations leading up to the implementation stage, they probably now have good insight into the need for the change and the reasons for the actions that are to be taken. If not, remedy this immediately. Examine the supervisor's knowledge of and disposition toward the change process. The supervisors can easily feel threatened by some aspects of the planned change. These views must be aired and addressed to ensure that the supervisors are fully enrolled as energetic supporters of the process.

Also, pay attention to building the skills required to supervise the new unit. Supervisors who have worked in unchanging operations will have little experience and skill in the management of change. Help and train them in areas like dealing with worker anxieties about change and helping work groups plan needed change elements. For most supervisors, the biggest and most difficult change will occur if the unit has decided to more fully empower workers. This challenging transition will require managerial support, training, and time.

In most organizations, information about the work processes flows directly to supervisors or managers who then make needed decisions and tell the workers what adjustments or actions are required. This system makes sense, and certainly makes the supervisors comfortable. Supervisors are in control of the work and have a clear sense of personal value and contribution.

Empowerment upsets all of this. It's the empowered workers who need the information and feedback about the work progress. They are the ones who need the analytical skill to properly evaluate the data, and the authority to act on the results of this analysis.

The supervisor is not needed to initiate or direct the work (the empowered employees do this themselves). Nor does the supervisor adjust the work processes and apply corrections. And, the workers themselves decide on actions so the supervisor is not required to direct. Therefore, the obvious question of just what is the job of the supervisor in an empowered employee situation arises.

Is Empowerment Good?

The empowerment of workers–providing them with more latitude and authority to do their jobs–is a popular trend, although its actual results are quite mixed. Establishing the proper nature and level of empowerment is a key in the process of building an effective internal service strategy.

Business school professors David Bowen and Edward Lawler investigated the characteristics that influence service firms to select different levels of empowerment for their employees. They examined successful companies like Club Med and American Express which have high employee empowerment. Their employees have the freedom, even the responsibility, to take independent actions to satisfy customer needs. But other successful companies like UPS, McDonald's, and Disney have chosen a way to deliver services that is very prescribed and routine with relatively low levels of independent initiative. They resemble a traditional production line. These successful service companies have chosen very different empowerment paths.

Bowen and Lawler determined which situations provided success with a "production line" approach and which produced good results with a more empowering approach.

Characteristics Which Favor a Production Line Approach		Characteristics Which Favor an Empowerment Approach
low cost, high volume	← BASIC BUSINESS STRATEGY →	differentiation, customization, personalized
transaction, short time period	← TIE TO CUSTOMER →	relationship, long time period
routine, simple	← TECHNOLOGY →	non-routine, complex
predictable, few surprises	← BUSINESS ENVIRONMENT →	unpredictable, many surprises
directive managers, employees with low growth needs, low social needs, and weak interpersonal skills	← TYPES OF PEOPLE →	participative managers, employees with high growth needs, high social needs, and strong interpersonal skills

SOURCE: David E. Bowen and Edward E. Lawler III, "The Empowerment of Service Workers: What, Why, How, and When," Sloan Management Review (Spring, 1992), pp. 31-39.

The old roles of authority figure, decision-maker, resource allocator, judge, and task-master disappear. Replacing these are more interpersonally challenging roles of coach, trainer, facilitator, and supporter. This fundamental role transition is difficult for nearly everyone, and impossible for many. Some empowerment efforts flounder because the program sounds great to top management, but the merits are less clear to first-line supervisors.

How supervisors obtain and use information about work system failures is another necessary reorientation, regardless of whether or not employees become more empowered. In most historical work systems, information about unsuccessful work outcomes (failures) has been used primarily for punishment and admonition—penalties come when negative feedback data appears. Quite naturally failures tend not to appear, whether or not they actually exist. (Workers aren't stupid!) Data about failures are buried, distorted, denied, and generally minimized. But *feedback about failures is essential to improvement* of service delivery processes. This means that in a true quality-oriented service system, the old way of looking at feedback about poor work results must be totally revised. Feedback, positive or negative, must be seen as useful, helpful, and vital. Everyone, supervisors and workers alike, must do all they can to help obtain and use all relevant feedback data. Therefore, *feedback on specific work outcomes can never be used for personal evaluation or penalty.* This is a big shift in thinking, particularly for supervisors. It requires some very specific training to accomplish motivation through means other than negative feedback.

Development of Work Teams

If more empowerment of workers is desired, then specific work teams need to be developed to foster this new function. Empowered work teams offer a powerful new resource but need to be created and supported with knowledge and skill. One of the best documented cases of significant turnaround using empowered work teams is the case of the NUMMI plant of General Motors in Fremont, California. Initial productivity was so low and problems were so severe that GM closed the plant in 1982. In 1986, GM decided to reopen the plant as a joint venture with Toyota, utilizing essentially the same work force, the same union, and the same equipment as before. But employee organization was very different. Workers were organized into small work teams, were retrained in work analysis and systems improvement, and were

The Dramatic NUMMI Turnaround

In 1963, General Motors opened a large automobile assembly plant in Freemont, California. The Freemont plant was organized along traditional production lines, but began experiencing many problems. Productivity was low, quality was abysmal, the plant had significant drug and alcohol abuse, and absenteeism was over 20 percent. GM-Freemont employed 6,800 hourly workers by 1978 but the problems continued to escalate. The plant was cited as "the worst plant in the world" when GM elected to close it in early 1982. It had been a frustrating twenty years.

In 1983, GM entered into a joint management agreement with Toyota in which it hoped to learn more about Japanese management techniques and the quality approach used by Toyota. The two companies would be partners on operating a plant—however, Toyota would be totally responsible for setting up and managing the production and work systems. The old GM plant at Freemont was selected as the site for the experiment and the New United Motor Manufacturing Corporation (NUMMI) was born.

Toyota upgraded some of the old Freemont equipment, but did not invest major capital in automation. Eighty percent of the newly hired NUMMI workers were old GM-Freemont workers—even the same UAW was retained. However, very dramatic changes were made in the way the people and work were organized. For example, instead of the old union contract with thousands of pages of fine print, the new NUMMI contract provided for only two categories of workers—"assemblers" and "technicians." Work analysis and revision were performed by teams of workers who received performance feedback directly (instead of through management) and executed needed changes. The plant utilized most of the quality techniques that had evolved.

The plant was up and running by the fall of 1986. The following results were obtained by 1987:

	GM (the old plant)	NUMMI FREEMONT	GM FRAMINGHAM (a typical GM plant in the U.S.)	TOYOTA TOKAOKA (a typical Toyota plant)
Assembly Hours/Car	43	19	31	16
Assembly Defects per 100 cars	140	45	135	45
Assembly Space per car (sq.ft.)		7.0	8.1	4.8
Average Inventory of Parts		2 days	2 weeks	2 hours

The results of the NUMMI experiment are dramatic, despite the fact that the only thing changed was the *method and approach of management*. Using essentially the same plant, the same workers, and the same union, strikingly different results were obtained. The quality approach had made a real difference.

SOURCES: Paul S. Adler, "Time-and-Motion Regained," *Harvard Business Review*, (Jan./Feb. 1993),97-108, and James P. Womack, Daniel T. Jones, and Daniel Roos, *The Machine That Changed the World*, New York, Macmillan, 1990.

charged with full responsibility for the effectiveness of their work unit. Considerable attention was also given to helping supervisors gain skill and comfort in coaching and facilitation roles. Many other changes were made to complement the new approach. By the end of 1986, NUMMI's productivity was higher than that of any other GM facility and more than twice that of the old NUMMI plant. In addition, quality was much higher than any other GM facility. Absenteeism had dropped from 25 percent to 4 percent, and 90 percent of the employees described themselves as "satisfied."

A central element in the NUMMI turnaround was the careful creation of a work force of truly empowered work teams—teams that had the tools, the skills, and the support to make real and substantive decisions about how their work would get done. While the payoffs of such a move for an organization are substantial, so are the necessary changes in approach and culture. Employees must be equipped with the skills and insights, as well as the current information, that they will need to make decisions about their work—and they must be empowered to make these decisions and take necessary corrective actions.

The payoff is a work system that drives decisions directly to the point where actual work is being done. Not only is the system more efficient, but service to customers is more personal and timely. The effort required for this degree of organizational change is substantial. Though difficult, the empowerment of teams can be a powerful tool to accomplish the implementation and improvement of internal service changes.

Linking Performance and Evaluation

Clear internal service unit performance standards link the overall evaluation and reward for the department to its performance. For individuals and teams, this stronger link promotes better focus on the performance goals. For managers, it means improved ability to use compensation, recognition, and promotion as further reinforcements for desired behaviors and accomplishments.

Redirect attention from activities to outcomes. After years of operation, many internal service units inadvertently slip into a primary focus on the specific activities that it takes to do its task, rather than on the final results it is trying to achieve. Input activities such as time spent answering customer calls, effort or money expended in developing system upgrades, or technical standards (all input activities) receive a lot of attention, and consequently, become the focus of evaluation. Results have been much more difficult to articulate, enumerate, and measure than input efforts. But the establishment of specific new service standards (output measures) permits a shift of attention from an internal focus to an external one. It generates renewed interest in finding out just what those final desired results are and how they could be measured. This change also forces a much tougher internal discipline on the unit. Clearer performance standards and measures facilitate this shift and permit direct links of the negotiated service standards to performance appraisal and evaluation.

Putting Chapter Sixteen Ideas to Work

Here are some questions to help promote thinking about how this material relates to your organization.

✓ In your internal service unit, how might work teams be employed most profitably? What opportunities for additional empowerment for teams exist? What cautions should be observed in this team empowerment process in your organization?

✓ How much interpersonal skill is now being evidenced by internal service personnel as they deal with customer unit people? Do customer unit people feel that they are getting respect and satisfaction at their "moments of truth?" Why do they feel this way?

✓ How empowered do the individual internal service personnel feel now? What causes them to feel less empowered? What could give them more sense of empowerment? What would be the result of more empowerment for them?

Chapter 17

The Ongoing Challenge

Building in Continuous Improvement

Internal service turnaround efforts and energies focus on very specific goals. Ironically, this can become a limitation to further progress as the unit accomplishes its goal. Unless the unit can learn to move beyond a specific goal, it can become fixed at that level. Once the initial turnaround nears completion, the internal service unit needs perspectives and mechanisms that enable it to continue to progress beyond the current goal.

In addressing personal growth, psychologist Carl Rogers has described a fully mature individual as one who constantly perceives himself to be in a "process of becoming," rather than in a "state of arriving." Throughout much of our life we have trained ourselves to set goals and strive for their achievement. This process, however, conditions us to focus on the goal and on the *state of arriving*. It detracts from our vision of the constant *process of becoming* something else which is really our destiny. Rogers emphasizes how much richer and fuller life can be if we shift to seeing ourselves as constantly in a process of transitioning, rather than always focusing on the next specific goal that we have set (and experiencing the difficult process of setting new goals once the original one has been achieved). This change of viewpoint dramatically changes how each of us sees our own purpose and life events.

Similarly, a healthy organization needs to see itself in a continuous state of evolving into something new, better, and more effective.

Specific goals are very important, but the overall self-concept must be one of building the *processes necessary for healthy change.* As the turnaround progresses, the unit leaves the doldrums of "beleaguered professional" and moves on through the stage of competent responder" and into "emerging excellence" (see Figure 1). But moving up to provide "world-class internal service" requires that the organization build processes to constantly renew itself and respond to the requirements and opportunities of a changing world. This approach to building in evolutionary capability is "continuous improvement."

Continuous improvement is more than a simple desire to do better. Most organizations have this desire, but few have built in the full internal processes, skills, and attitudes that are necessary to support real continuous improvement.

The emerging excellent internal service unit anticipates customer needs, and the world-class internal service unit learns and improves competency and customer need insights. Both of these must stay attuned to changing external environments that might change customers' needs and sometimes necessitate the need for new service standards, or changing levels of acceptability.

Certainly rapid technology changes are altering both service needs and service provider capabilities. New needs and solutions have emerged, for example, as information technology provides computer information transmission by radio link. Otis Elevator uses this new capability to provide its maintenance people immediate on-site access to all maintenance data on every Otis elevator in the country. First Commerce Corporation created state-of-the-art computer links to New Orleans riverboat casinos to provide safe and secure ATM capabilities in wireless transmissions. All of this requires the capability to stay attuned to and adapt to changing customer needs, changing environmental factors, and new technologies.

Learning is a key capability in a continuous improvement culture. Learning vs. static internal service cultures differ greatly on their *values* and *behavior*. The following chart contrasts the values and behavior for these two types:

Alternative Service Cultures

	Learning Culture	Static Culture
Values	- Managers concerned with customer needs, people, and processes that can lead to service improvements are highly valued; learning and adaptivity emphasized	- Most managers concerned with themselves, their immediate work group, or some specific product or technology associated with that work group; they value orderly, risk-minimizing efforts
Behavior	- Managers stay attuned to all constituencies (customers, employees, stakeholders) by ensuring open flows of information and need-sharing; they initiate change when appropriate, even if some risks involved; they take responsibility for success of relationships with customer units and stakeholders	- Managers insulate themselves politically and bureaucratically; they are slow to adjust or change strategies or services as a reaction to changing business environments; communications with outsiders limited

For many internal service cultures, the bureaucratic, political, and insular characteristics of the static culture may be all too familiar. The opportunity to build learning elements into the new internal service unit culture provides the exciting prospect of long-term viability and effectiveness.

The objective, then, for long-term organizational success, is to build a real learning organization that has adaptive mechanisms to gather on-going data about the needs it is trying to serve, and the effectiveness of its processes for meeting those needs. Develop an internal ability to learn and evolve as the situation changes. The internal service organization completing a performance renaissance has probably earned the organizational time and resources that it needs to make this next big step.

A "Critical Success Factors" Checklist

Many parts of this book have examined individual aspects of creating a turnaround in internal service unit performance. The elements that are most essential to achieving effectiveness in a turnaround in internal service performance are the *critical success factors* for that process—the factors that absolutely must be done right to produce overall success in the organizational change.

Every organization has attempted various change efforts; some ended in success, more probably ended in failure and frustration. Examination of why past change efforts failed or succeeded is a key to future change success. This is a practical way to identify those variables that transcend the details and must receive paramount focus and attention throughout the change process if it is to be successful and permanent. This list provides an excellent last check before implementation:

- Make the need for change salient.
- Solidify support from the top.
- Be bold: challenge your paradigm.
- Use a planned approach to organizational change.
- Anticipate resistances.
- Keep power in balance.
- Involve the customer in the change process.
- Measure, measure, measure.

Each of these topics has been explored earlier in the book but are presented here as a way to formally check your state of readiness.

1. *Make the need for change salient.* The need for a change comes before planning and must be fully understood and broadly felt. Inadequate attention here condemns many organizational change processes to mediocre, or worse, results. As an organization feels intense pain about some poorly functioning element, it is tempting to rush quickly to relieve this pain. Action at this point is almost always oriented at removing the symptoms, not the real causes. A quick fix temporarily relieves some of the immediate pain and allows the organization to get back to work. But if the real problem is not addressed, pain reoccurs. The organization will again have to marshal resources to deal with it, and the effort will have drained needed energy for reform. This cycle repeatedly occurs until a more substantive approach to the problem is taken.

2. *Solidify support from the top.* A second temptation is to ask your CEO for a blessing to "go fix it." A CEO with only a superficial sense of the organizational pain around an internal service problem may be tempted to offer quick authorization. The apparent remedy may be launched quickly, but will then

encounter obstacles or resource needs that were unforeseen and unanticipated by the CEO. This produces a dilemma for the change agent—whether to go back and explain the need for the change in direction, or simply to proceed under the assumption that the initial general authorization was broad enough to cover the new situation and need. Either way, the CEO's expectations are likely to be violated—a definite problem. If the CEO has gained a full understanding of the real need prior to authorizing action, the chances for continued support from the top throughout the project increase dramatically.

Further solidify this support by providing on-going progress reports and communication with top management about the process. Communications at regular intervals can be used to sense any emerging violation of expectations, as well as to inform.

3. *Be bold: challenge your paradigm.* Over the years, every organization establishes specific ways of looking at its world, its customers, and its processes. This paradigm, or framework, provides the organization with a helpful way of thinking about itself and its work—it is used to socialize new members and to help existing ones do their job. But it also limits and constrains thinking. When asked to improve performance, almost everyone starts to fine-tune details within their existing organizational paradigm. But in many cases, the paradigm itself is wrong, very limiting, or has not evolved with changing conditions. Challenge the fundamental paradigm itself to achieve real progress.

   Decide early whether this change is to be a minor adjustment, or a fundamental shift. These two alternatives require very different change strategies. For example, if customer awareness is not a core value in the existing culture, it cannot be inserted by simple adjustments. This is a major and fundamental shift in focus, requiring a commensurate change strategy.

4. *Use a planned approach to organizational change.* Turning around an internal service unit is a complex and difficult process. Because it deals with interpersonal and cultural variables, however, it is often viewed as not requiring the level of detailed planning required in more concrete mechanical processes. Even

though the variables may be more abstract, the required planning detail does not diminish. An organized approach uses an appropriate overall framework, and plans the detail of individual elements carefully. One of the most general organizational change models is also one of the simplest:

- Understand the current state. Examine and understand in detail the current situation, the existing organizational functioning, and the need for change.
- Visualize the desired future state. Construct a specific vision of the desired future outcomes and carefully articulate the setting and the organization that would be necessary to produce them.
- Plan the necessary transition elements. Plan the detail of the overall framework and the individual elements that would be necessary to get "from here to there."

Use a systematic approach to the change process to ensure that the inherent complexity of the changes are accommodated in the plan resulting in fewer surprises along the way and a much higher probability that the change is effective and permanent.

5. *Anticipate resistances*. Any change process encounters resistances. They might be from customers, from members of top management, from other internal service units, or from the members of the unit itself. You don't control the existence of these resistances, but you do control how effectively they are dealt with. You can more effectively handle an *anticipated resistance* than one which is unanticipated. Create a state of empathy with all stakeholders and identify, in advance, the nature and causes of the various types of resistances that may be encountered in the project. Then plot out a strategy to accommodate and deal with them appropriately and effectively.

6. *Keep power in balance.* Power is a key variable in internal service effectiveness. Before a turnaround, many internal service units may have excessive power and use it to bludgeon their customers. Or, the customer units may be bludgeoning the service unit. A turnaround rebalances that power and moves the relationship to one of a partnership—a partnership with relatively equal power between customer and service supplier, but with very different responsibilities and competencies.

A risk is that power can shift too far in redressing an imbalance. The customer unit may misinterpret openness on the part of the service unit as weakness and move to satisfy their service needs through power dominance. Or, the service unit could find new strength in success and strive to dominate the customer units.

A partnership in the production of service excellence requires a balance in power. Although responsibility for keeping the power balance at appropriate levels ultimately falls to the CEO, the organizational change agent or manager in an internal service situation should remain very aware of it.

7. *Involve the customer in the change process.* Key representatives of the customer units can provide important insights and perspectives and certainly have an interest in the success of the change process. The process initiative lies with the internal service unit, but customer input and involvement provide needed information, useful liaison contacts, and act as a discipline to the overall process. In addition, customer representatives who have been an integral part of the change process become valuable influence and information agents within their own units regarding the nature and progress of the change processes. If these customer representatives are treated with respect and are viewed as valuable sources of perspective, they certainly will become advocates of the process within their own units.

8. *Measure, measure, measure.* Any successful change process must have a method for measuring specific service processes and outcomes. The results of having such a system in place are:
   - Customer expectations are clarified.
   - Unrealistic expectations are confronted in advance.
   - Key service variables are identified.
   - Specific measures are negotiated.
   - Responsibility for fixing service problems is moved closer to contact personnel.
   - Discussions with customers about service become issue-centered, not person-centered.

Implementation of a turnaround change is one of the most sensitive portions of the entire process because much of the effort is so closely linked to the people who execute it. The culture they work in, their own ability to function as service people, and the supervision that they receive, can provide strong support, or resistance, to the process. Aligning these human factors with the organizational change and building in a capability for continuous improvement are significant challenges to implementation.

The Internal Service Challenge

In the coming decades the internal service organization will be subjected to much higher standards of corporate contribution. Its monopoly position coupled with the difficulty of service measurement has partially insulated it from the extreme competitive pressures experienced by line units. But measurement is improving, benchmarking provides direct comparison data, and outsourcing is a viable option. The insulation is disappearing. Some units will see this increased contribution pressure as a call to strengthen their defenses and insularity. But others will see the broader challenge and work to integrate themselves as full corporate partners.

Each internal service unit will choose its own fate, either explicitly or by default. Each will be condemned to a never-ending holding action against complaints and challenges by disgruntled customer units and frustrated top management, or it may work to become part of the highly contributing vanguard of corporate partnership. Action, or inaction, on this choice casts the shape of the future for the internal service unit. What will it be for your organization?

Putting Chapter Seventeen Ideas to Work

Here are questions to help promote thinking about how this material relates to your organization.

✓ Is a philosophy of "continuous improvement" part of your organization's recent history? How much have the internal service units been involved with this type of thinking?

✓ It is very difficult to move an organization that has been obsessed with survival and coping into a real learning culture in which the goals are to become better and more adaptive. What forces or allies might be available to you as you try to create a learning culture within your organization?

✓ In your organizational change process, what are the major application problems and issues associated with each of the critical success factors below:

- Make the need for change salient.
- Solidify support from the top.
- Be bold: challenge your paradigm.
- Use a planned approach to organizational change.
- Anticipate resistances.
- Keep power in balance.
- Involve the customer in the change process.
- Measure, measure, measure.

Endnotes

Chapter One

1. James L. Heskett, Thomas O. Jones, Gary W. Loveman, W. Earl Sasser, Jr., and Leonard Schlesinger, "Putting the Service-Profit Chain to Work," *Harvard Business Review*, March/April 1994, p. 165.

Chapter Two

1. Peter F. Drucker, "Sell the Mailroom," *The Wall Street Journal,* July 25, 1969, p. A16.

2. Jason Magidon and Andrew E. Polcha, "Creating Market Economics Within Companies," *Journal of Business Stategy*, May/June 1992, p. 39.

Chapter Five

1. Jason Magidon and Andrew E. Polcha, "Creating Market Economics Within Companies," *Journal of Business Stategy*, 13, May/June 1992, p. 41.

2. *Ibid.*

3. Bruce Pfau, Denis Detzel, and Andrew Geller, "Satisfy Your Internal Customer," *The Journal of Business Strategy,* November/December 1991, p. 11.

Chapter Ten

1. Peter F. Drucker, "The Theory of Business," *Harvard Business Review,* September/October 1994, pp. 95–104.

2. Karl Albrecht, *Service Within*, Richard D. Irwin, Homewood, Illinois, 1990, p. 56.

3. CE Roundtable, "Can't Get No (Customer) Satisfaction...," *Chief Executive*, September/October 1989, p. 78.

Chapter Twelve

1. George P. Bohan and Nicholas F. Horney, "Pinpointing the Real Cost of Quality in a Service Company," *National Productivity Review*, Summer 1991, p. 309.

2. Shiomo Maital, "When You Absolutely, Positively Have to Give Better Service," *Across the Board*, Vol. 28, March, 1991, p. 8.

Chapter Thirteen

1. R. L. Nolan, "Effects of Chargeout on User/Management Attitudes," *Communications of the ACM*, 13:8, March, 1977, p 180.

Chapter Fifteen

1. John P. Kotter and James L. Heskett, *Corporate Culture and Performance*, New York, Free Press, 1992, pp. 19–27.

Appendix A

Diagnosing the State of Current Service

Survey Instruments and Interview Format

Much of Part IV focuses on how to collect the pertinent information you will need to design a substantive action plan. This appendix contains the analytical tools that a change-planning team may use in gathering the information needed to engineer an internal service unit renaissance.

Let's begin by reviewing the steps to take to obtain information about current service.

1. *Solidify the change team.* Once the specific team responsible or the overall change process has been identified, it must solidify its own objectives and approach.
2. *Survey the change team.* An internal survey like the one presented in this appendix can be used to help the members of the change team articulate their collective views of the impending change process and to form a needed consensus regarding action.
3. *Identify key stakeholders and customer representatives.* It is usually impractical to gather data from the entire customer population. Therefore, for this and other subsequent processes, it is important to identify a smaller number of key individuals in each customer unit (perhaps two to five persons per customer unit). These individuals should have the greatest input on service delivery decisions and interact consistently with the internal service unit.

4. *Gain support for solicitation of data.* The individuals who will be solicited for input need to understand the reasons for the request and the seriousness of the overall effort. It will be important to gain their understanding and cooperation *before* they see any specific questionnaire or survey. This can be accomplished through a carefully planned meeting focused on this process.

5 *Administer the survey.* A customer survey is included in this appendix. If you are going to design your own survey, it would be useful to think ahead to the time when you will be designing the final performance measurement systems for your unit and incorporate these elements here in order to obtain crucial base line data on key variables.

6. *Conduct in-depth interviews.* The survey instrument will provide a reliable perspective on current service. However, the change team will also need detailed insight into the perceived service needs of the customer units, and the precise service expectations that now exist. These are best covered in a series of one-on-one interviews with key customer unit representatives. The change team should conduct the interviews. It's important that they remain objective and resist the temptation to counter and argue with customers at this point. A suggested interview outline is included in this appendix.

7. *Follow-up.* Once the data is gathered, its primary use will be to help the change team better understand the current state of its relationship with customer units. However, communication (or the lack of it) with the customer units following the survey could set the tone for future interactions. Share the data with customer units and key stakeholders and be gracious toward them for cooperating in the data-gathering effort.

(To be filled out only by members of this department)
Internal Service Survey for Members of the _____ Department

We are in the process of launching a process designed to improve the service that our department delivers to its customer units. To begin this effort we need to understand, among other things, how we now see the current process of rendering service. Please take a few moments to answer the questions below. Your answers will be held in confidence. For each question, please circle the response that represents your perspective. Thank you.

Understanding Our Customer's Needs

In order for us to serve customer units within the company effectively, we must have a good understanding of their service needs. On a scale of 1 to 5, with 1 being poor and 5 being excellent (DK - "Don't Know," and NA - "Not Applicable"), please rate our department's current performance on:

POOR   EXCELLENT

1. Including customer needs in service design and delivery   1 2 3 4 5   DK   NA

2. Utilizing effective methods for learning customer needs   1 2 3 4 5   DK   NA

3. Responding quickly to changing customer needs   1 2 3 4 5   DK   NA

4. Being truly "customer driven"   1 2 3 4 5   DK   NA

Service Quality

Please rate our department's current performance on:

POOR   EXCELLENT

5. Having "excellence in service" as a prime internal focus

1 2 3 4 5   DK NA

6. Possessing the needed technical competence and expertise

1 2 3 4 5   DK NA

7. Incorporating quality assurance techniques into all service creation

1 2 3 4 5   DK NA

8. Delivering excellent service quality to customers

1 2 3 4 5   DK NA

Cost-Sensitivity

Please rate our department's current performance on:

POOR   EXCELLENT

9. Having internal processes that emphasize cost control

1 2 3 4 5   DK NA

10. Offering services at a lower cost than could be obtained on the outside

1 2 3 4 5   DK NA

11. "Editing out" marginal value services that drive costs up

1 2 3 4 5   DK NA

12. Delivering service at low cost

1 2 3 4 5   DK NA

Responsiveness

Please rate our department's current performance on:

POOR   EXCELLENT

13. Dealing with customers in an
    open and positive manner

    1 2 3 4 5   DK   NA

14. Being prompt in responding
    to requests

    1 2 3 4 5   DK   NA

15. Recovering quickly when service
    problems occur

    1 2 3 4 5   DK   NA

16. Being responsive to the needs and
    issues of customer units

    1 2 3 4 5   DK   NA

The Need for Change

Please rate our department's current need for change.

LOW   HIGH

17. How strongly do our customer
    units want us to change?

    1 2 3 4 5   DK   NA

18. How strongly does top management
    want us to change?

    1 2 3 4 5   DK   NA

19. How much could we improve our
    efficiency and effectiveness if we
    had better relations with customer
    units?

    1 2 3 4 5   DK   NA

20. How strong is the need to
    fundamentally restructure how our
    department renders service?

    1 2 3 4 5   DK   NA

(To be filled out by customer unit personnel and key stakeholders)

Customer Questionnaire

The _____ Department is determined to improve service to its customers within the company and is launching a major effort to do so. If we are to plan truly effective improvements, we must base this plan on a solid and realistic assessment of the current situation. You are a key individual in our interactions and we need your input and perspective to help us begin our analysis. Please take a few moments to answer the following questions. Your answers will be held in confidence. For each question, please circle the number that represents your perspective on the _____ Department. Thank you.

Understanding Our Customer's Needs

In order for us to serve our customer units within the company effectively, we must have a good understanding of their service needs. On a scale of 1 to 5 with 1 being poor and 5 being excellent (DK - "Don't Know," and NA - "Not Applicable"), please rate our department's current performance on:

	POOR				EXCELLENT		
1. Including customer needs in service design and delivery	1	2	3	4	5	DK	NA
2. Utilizing effective methods for learning customer needs	1	2	3	4	5	DK	NA
3. Responding quickly to changing customer needs	1	2	3	4	5	DK	NA
4. Being truly "customer-driven"	1	2	3	4	5	DK	NA

Service Quality

Please rate our department's current performance on:

	POOR				EXCELLENT		
5. Having "excellence in service" as a prime internal focus	1	2	3	4	5	DK	NA

6. Possessing technical competence
   and expertise   1 2 3 4 5   DK   NA

7. Incorporating quality assurance
   techniques into all service
   creation   1 2 3 4 5   DK   NA

8. Delivering excellent service
   quality to customers   1 2 3 4 5   DK   NA

Cost-Sensitivity

Please rate our department's current performance on:

POOR   EXCELLENT

9. Having internal processes that
   emphasize cost control   1 2 3 4 5   DK   NA

10. Offering services at a lower cost
    than could be obtained on the outside   1 2 3 4 5   DK   NA

11. "Editing out" marginal value
    services that drive costs up   1 2 3 4 5   DK   NA

12. Delivering service at low cost   1 2 3 4 5   DK   NA

Responsiveness

Please rate our department's current performance on:

POOR   EXCELLENT

13. Dealing with customers in an
    open and positive manner   1 2 3 4 5   DK   NA

14. Being prompt in responding
    to requests   1 2 3 4 5   DK   NA

15. Recovering well when service
    problems occur   1 2 3 4 5   DK   NA

16. Being responsive to the needs and
    issues of customer units   1 2 3 4 5   DK   NA

The Need for Change

Please rate our department's current need for change.

	LOW				HIGH		
17. How strongly do our customer units want us to change?	1	2	3	4	5	DK	NA
18. How strongly does top management want us to change?	1	2	3	4	5	DK	NA
19. How much could we improve our efficiency and effectiveness if we had better relations with customer units?	1	2	3	4	5	DK	NA
20. How strong is the need to fundamentally restructure how our department renders service?	1	2	3	4	5	DK	NA

Please list any other comments concerning the service you receive from the _____ Department in the space below:

_____

_____

_____

_____

_____

_____

Name _____ (optional)

Department _____ (optional)

Thank you for your help, please return this completed form to

_____

Customer Interview Format

To gain the most information from customer units, you may want to conduct personal interviews with key customer representatives and/or stakeholders.

In the interviews, the interviewer's skill and approach is instrumental in determining the quality and objectivity of the data obtained. In order for the information to be valuable to the change team, it must represent the actual and candid perspective of the interviewee. The views and opinions of the interviewer must remain out of this process or the data will be too tainted to be of use.

The questions in the suggested interview format are open-ended, that is, they require the interviewee to think about his or her thoughts on the subject and then construct a candid answer. Obviously, if the interviewer "winces" at negative responses or argues with interviewees about their assumptions or viewpoints, the answers received will be guarded. Instead, follow-up on comments made by the interviewee with thoughtful and nonaccusatory requests for further explanation. This will set the stage for a positive exchange of useful information.

For example, what would be the effect of the following exchange?

Interviewer: "What do you consider the most serious problem affecting the interaction between the service unit and your department?"

Customer: "Your department is always very slow in responding to information requests. In our department we are on a tight schedule and this really sets us back."

Interviewer: "But we find that most of your data requests are poorly formulated. We always have to go back and nail down exactly what is wanted. If we didn't have to do that, then our service could be really fast."

In contrast, what would be the effect of this exchange if the interviewer's response was this:

Interviewer: "Waiting for a response can be exasperating. Is there some particular type or class of information request that seems to be causing the most trouble on turnaround time?"

Obviously, the first reply provokes a combative relationship. The interviewee will be hesitant about providing candid answers. The second response, on the other hand, motivates the interviewee to be open and to elaborate on their perspective. It is difficult in the midst of an actual interview to remain objective. But don't try to correct poor impressions now—there will be better opportunity for that later.

One last thing before you proceed with the interviews: Make sure you understand the distinction between "needs" and "expectations." *Needs* are the basic requirements of the customer department. In the interviews, it is important to help customer unit representatives articulate their views of the needs of their department as they relate to the internal service unit. *Expectations* are views held by customers about how their needs can and should be satisfied by the internal service unit. These are subject to broad interpretation. The needs are inherent in the situation. The expectations are viewpoints of how the needs should be met.

Part of the interview is directed at uncovering the basic underlying service needs of the customer unit. Other portions are focused on revealing the more general expectations they have about service. Following is an interview outline that can be used to obtain data on needs and expectations.

Interview Outline for
Key Customer Representatives

Person Interviewed _____ Department _____

Date of Interview _____ Interviewed by _____

The Nature of Your Experience with the _____
Department

1. Describe the situations in which you most often come in contact
   with or use the services of the _____ Department.

   _____

   _____

   _____

   _____

2. Which of these service interactions have been most positive from
   your perspective as a customer?

   _____

   _____

   _____

   _____

3. Which ones have been the most negative?

   _____

   _____

   _____

   _____

Your Perception of Basic Service Needs

("Needs" refer to this customer's basic underlying needs for service. These needs belong to and are attached to the customer unit, regardless of how well or how poorly the internal service unit may meet them.)

4. What are the top two or three service needs (within the service purview of the _____ Department) that your department has?

_____

_____

_____

5. What other, less crucial needs (again, within the purview of the _____ Department) does your department have?

_____

_____

_____

Your Service Expectations

("Expectations" refer to the view that this individual has about how service should be delivered to meet the unit's needs.)

6. What are the specific service expectations that you have regarding the way service should be provided by the _____ Department? (What kind of services are expected? Where, when, and how are they provided? At what cost? etc.)

_____

_____

_____

_____

7. In what specific ways does the _____ Department meet or exceed these expectations now?

_____

_____

_____

8. In what specific ways does the _____ Department fail to meet these expectations now?

_____

_____

_____

General Comments

9. What could the _____ Department do to gain additional insights into the real service needs of your department?

_____

_____

_____

10. What else would you like to add that might help us better understand your service needs and expectations?

_____

_____

_____

_____

_____

_____

Appendix B

Baldrige Award Winners

In 1987, President Ronald Reagan established the annual U.S. National Quality Award. It is designed to promote quality awareness, recognize quality achievements of U.S. companies, and to publicize successful quality strategies. The program is managed by the Secretary of Commerce and the National Institute of Standards and Technology. Not more than two awards are presented in each of three categories:

- Manufacturing companies or subsidiaries
- Service companies or subsidiaries
- Small business (independently owned and fewer than 500 full-time employees)

A Resource for Internal Service Organizations

Any winner of the Baldrige Award pledges to share quality-related information with other U.S. companies that may seek it. This becomes a treasure trove for internal service organizations looking for direct comparative benchmarking data and innovative and effective ideas for various service processes.

BALDRIGE WINNERS

Manufacturing Category
1995
Corning, Inc., Telecommunications Products Division
Contact: Gerald J. McQuaid,
Division Vice President
Corning, NY 14831
Telephone: (800) 525-2524, ext. 30, fax: (607) 754-7517

1995

Armstrong World Industries, Inc., Building Products Operations
Contact: John F. McClay,
Manager, Quality Management
313 West Liberty Street
Lancaster, PA 17603
Telephone: (717) 396-2540, fax: (717) 396-3304

1993

Eastman Chemical Company
Contact: Katherine Watkins,
Advanced Sales Support Specialist
P.O. Box 431
Kingsport, TN 37662-5350
Telephone: 1(800)695-4322, ext. 1150, fax: (615)229-1195

1992

AT&T Network Systems Group, Transmission Systems
Business Unit
Contact: Louis E. Monteforte,
Director, Transmission Quality Planning
475 South Street, Room 2W-44
Morristown, NJ 07962-1976
Telephone: (201)606-2488, fax: (201)606-3363

1992

Texas Instruments, Defense Systems & Electronics Group
Contact: (no name available)
P.O. Box 660246
MS 3124
Dallas, TX 75266
Fax: (214) 480-4880

1991

Solectron Corporation
Contact: Margaret Smith
Marketing Program Specialist
847 Gibraltar Drive
Milpitas, CA 95035
Telephone: (408)956-6768, fax: (408)956-6056

1991

Zytec Corporation
Contact: Karen Scheldroup
Baldrige Office
7575 Market Place Drive
Eden Prairie, MN 5534
Telephone: (612)941-1100, ext. 104, fax: (612)829-1837

1990

Cadillac Motor Car Company
Contact: Joseph R. Bransky,
Director, Quality and Reliability, General Motors Corporation
General Motors Building, Rm. 6-162
Detroit, MI 48202
Telephone: (313)556-9050, fax: (313)974-6899

1990

IBM Rochester
Contact: IBM Rochester
Center for Excellence
3605 Highway 52 North
Rochester, MN 55901-7829
Telephone: (507)253-9000, fax:(507)253-4461

1989

Milliken & Company
Contact: Craig Long
Director of Quality
P.O. Box 1926, M-186
Spartanburg, SC 29304
Telephone: (803)573-2003, fax: (803)573-2505
Tours: Sandra Howell, (803)573-1988

1989

Xerox Business Products and Systems
Contact: John G. Lawrence,
Manager, Quality Communications Office
1387 Fairport Road, Building 1100
Fairport, NY 14450
Telephone: (716)383-7502, fax: (716)383-7517

1988

Motorola, Inc.
Contact: Richard Buetow,
Senior Vice President and Director of Quality
1303 East Algonquin Road
Schaumburg, IL 60196
Telephone: (708)576-5516, fax: (708)538-2663

1988

Westinghouse Commercial Nuclear Fuel Division
Contact: Carl Arendt,
Manager, Communications Productivity and Quality Center
P.O. Box 160
Pittsburgh, PA 15230-0160
Telephone: (412)778-5008, fax: (412)778-5153

Service Category

1994

AT&T Consumer Communications Services
Contact: Diane Phelp-Feldkamp,
Director, Quality and Business Improvement
295 N. Maple Avenue, Room 6356F3
Basking Ridge, NJ 07920
Telephone: (800)473-5047, fax: (904)636-3780

1994

GTE Directories Corporation
Contact: Jim Runyon,
Director, Quality Services
GTE Place, West Airfield Drive
P.O. Box 619810
D/FW Airport, TX 75261-9810
Telephone: (214)453-7985, fax: (214)453-6785

1992
AT&T Universal Card Services
Contact: Greg Swindell,
Chief Quality Officer
8787 Baypine Road, Room 3-2-151N
Jacksonville, FL 32256
Telephone: (904)954-8897, fax: (904)954-7118
Tours: (800)682-7759

1992
The Ritz-Carlton Hotel Company
Contact: Patrick Mene,
Vice President of Quality
3414 Peachtree Road, N.E., Suite 300
Atlanta, GA 30326
Telephone: (404)237-5500, fax: (404)261-0119

1990
Federal Express Corporation
Contact: Jean Ward-Jones,
Manager, Corporate Quality
P.O. Box 727
Memphis, TN 38194-2142
Telephone: (901)395-4539, fax: (901)395-4641

Small Business Category

1994
Wainwright Industries
Contact: Michael Simms,
Plant Manager
P.O. Box 640
St. Peters, MO 63376
Telephone: (314)278-5850, fax: (314)278-8806

1993

Ames Rubber Corporation
Contact: Charles A. Roberts
Vice President, Total Quality
23-47 Ames Boulevard
Hamburg, NJ 07419
Telephone: (201)209-3200, fax: (201)827-8893

1992

Granite Rock Company
Contact: Bruce W. Woolpert,
President and CEO
P.O. Box 50001
Watsonville, CA 95077-5001
Telephone: (408)761-2300, fax: (408)724-3484

1991

Marlow Industries
Contact: Tiki Miller,
Baldrige Activities Coordinator
10451 Vista Park Road
Dallas, TX 75238-1645
Telephone: (214)340-4900

1990

Wallace Company, Inc.
Contact: Wilson Industries
(Wallace Company has been acquired by Wilson Industries)
1302 Conti
Houston, TX 77002
Telephone: (713)237-3700, fax: (713)237-5935

1988

Globe Metallurgical, Inc.
Contact: Norman Jennings,
Quality Director
P.O. Box 157
Beverly, OH 45715
Telephone: (614)984-2361, fax: (614)984-8635

Appendix C

Selected Reading on Internal Service Excellence

Additional sources of information on improving internal service performance are organized here by book part.

PART I: THE INTERNAL SERVICE CRISIS

Drucker, Peter F. "The New Productivity Challenge." *Harvard Business Review* (November/December 1991), pp. 69-79.
  - *Explores the relative stagnation of service worker productivity and the importance and possible methodology of a remedy.*

Lee, Chris. "The Customer Within." *Training* (July 1991), pp. 21-26.
  - *Contains many good examples of the importance of well-functioning internal service organizations.*

Pfau, Bruce, Dennis Detzel, and Andrew Geller. "Satisfy Your Internal Customers." *The Journal of Business Strategy* (November/December 1991), pp. 9-13.
  - *Describes the importance of an effective internal customer focus and the consequences for the external customer if it exists.*

Porter, Michael E., *Competitive Advantage: Creating and Sustaining Superior Performance*, The Free Press, New York, 1985.
  - *Discusses the concept of the value chain, particularly as it applies to service organizations.*

Rothchild, Michael. "Coming Soon: Internal Markets." *Forbes ASAP* (June 7, 1993), pp. 19-21.
  - *Shows how frustration with poorly functioning internal service organizations is creating pressure to build real markets in which full costs and outside competitors for internal services is the norm.*

Sellers, Patricia. "Companies That Service You Best." *Fortune* (May 31, 1993), pp. 74-88.
- *Lists the best service organizations in twelve industries based on interviews with seventy-five consultants, business leaders, and executives.*

PART II: THE FORCES AT WORK

Albrecht, Karl, and Ron Zemke. *Service America,* New York, NY, Warner Books, 1990.
- *Provides an early examination of the problems of service organizations and how they might be addressed.*

Bitran, Gabriel R. and Johannes Hoech. "The Humanization of Service: Respect at the Moment of Truth." *Sloan Management Review* (Winter 1990), pp. 89-96.
- *An excellent exploration of the role of power in the service encounter.*

Handy, Charles. "Balancing Corporate Power: A New Federalist Paper." *Harvard Business Review* (November/December 1992), pp. 59-72.
- *Explores the internal organizational struggle between centralized corporate power (often held in internal service organizations) and decentralized power in field units is thoughtfully explored in this article.*

Harrell, Gilbert D., and Matthew F. Fors. "Internal Marketing of a Service." *Industrial Marketing Management*, 21 (November 1992), pp. 299-306.
- *Describes a case study on specific methods of marketing internal services to others within the same firm.*

Lacity, Mary C., Leslie P. Willcocks, and David F. Feeny, "I T Outsourcing: Maximize Flexibility and Control." *Harvard Business Review,* (May/June, 1995), pp. 84-93.
- *Reports on an excellent study that highlights the variables of flexibility and control—elements that may be even more meaningful than the traditional strategic dimensions.*

PART III: ASSESSMENT/COMMITMENT

Albrecht, Karl. *Service Within: Solving the Middle Management Leadership Crisis* Homewood, IL, Richard D. Irwin, 1990.
- *Describes, in a candid way, the problems and issues of internal service organizations. Its material is largely derived from an earlier book that Albrecht completed with Ron Zemke, Service America!, Warner Books, New York, 1985.*

Coyne, Kevin P. "Achieving a Sustainable Service Advantage." *Journal of Business Strategy,* 14 (January/February 1993), pp. 3-10.
- *Takes a strategic perspective in examining how excellence in aspects of service delivery can be the source of long-term competitive advantage.*

Duck, Jeanie Daniel. "Managing Change: The Art of Balancing." *Harvard Business Review* (November/December 1993), pp. 109-118.
- *Presents a good overview of some of the issues and traps inherent in executing large organizational changes.*

Heskett, J.L., Thomas O. Jones, Gary Loveman, W. Earl Sasser, Jr., and Leonard A. Schlesinger. "Putting the Service-Profit Chain to Work." *Harvard Business Review* (March/April 1994), pp. 164-174.
- *Elaborates on the sequential steps of adding value in a service organization.*

Kotter, John P., "Leading Changes: Why Transformation Efforts Fail." *Harvard Business Review,* March/April 1995, pp. 59-67.
- *Reviews the factors that can impede effectiveness in organizational change efforts.*

Schlesinger, Leonard A., and James L. Heskett. "The Service-Driven Company." *Harvard Business Review* (September/October 1993), pp. 71-81.
- *Questions traditional management premises. It sparked considerable controversy (addressed in the following issue of HBR, November/December, 1991, pp. 146-158).*

Schlesinger, Leonard A., and James L. Heskett. "Breaking the Cycle of Failure in Services." *Sloan Management Review,* (Spring 1991), pp. 17-28.
- *Provides several examples of bumping up pay levels to get more performance from service workers.*

Shapiro, Benson P. "What the Hell is 'Market Oriented'?" *Harvard Business Review,* (November/December 1988), pp. 119-125.
- *Explores the trials of a company attempting to move to a market orientation, but first needing to find out just what that means.*

Zemke, Ron with Dick Schaaf. *The Service Edge: 101 Companies That Profit from Customer Care,* Plume, New York, NY, 1990.
- *Presents case histories of 101 companies that provide exemplary service.*

PART IV: INFORMATION GATHERING

Brown, T.J., et.al. "The Measurement of Service Quality." *Journal of Retailing*, 69 (Spring 1993), pp. 127-147.
- *Describes the SERVQUAL scale has been developed over several years as a device to measure service quality. This academic article explores improvement/use of this scale.*

Drucker, Peter F., "The Theory of the Business." *Harvard Business Review*, September/October 1994, pp. 95-104.
- *Describes the key role of the underlying assumptions used by members of a business unit.*

Maital, Shiomo, "When You Absolutely, Positively Have to Give Better Service." *Across The Board*, 28 (March 1991), pp. 8-12.
- *Describes a quality tracking system used by Federal Express to gain timely insights into needed system changes.*

Welch, James F. "Service Quality Measurement at American Express Traveler's Cheque Group." *National Productivity Review*, 11, no. 4 (Fall 1992), pp. 463-471.
- *Looks at the quality principles and the service quality measurement system used at American Express Traveler's Cheque Group.*

Wilkerson, David, and Jefferson Kellogg. "Quantifying the Soft Stuff: How to Select the Assessment Tool You Need." *Employment Relations Today* (Winter 1992/93), pp. 413-424.
- *Compares a variety of morale surveys, attitude surveys, climate surveys, and cultural assessments aimed at helping get the right assessment tool for the task.*

PART V: BUILDING THE ACTION PLAN

Berry, Leonard L., Valarie A. Zeithaml, and A. Parasuraman. "Five Imperatives for Improving Service Quality." *Sloan Management Review*, 31 (Summer 1990), pp. 29-38.
- *Reviews the importance of tangibles, reliability, responsiveness, assurance, and empathy in producing excellent performance in service organizations.*

Bowen, David E. and Benjamin Schneider, "Boundary Spanning Role Employees and the Service Encounter: Some Guidelines for Management and Research." *The Service Encounter*, J. A. Czepiel, et. al., editors, D. C. Heath, Lexington, MA, 1985.
- *Discusses the issue of establishing and utilizing boundary spanning employees.*

Camp, Robert C., *BENCHMARKING: The Search for Industry Best Practices that Lead to Superior Performance*, Quality Press, Milwaukee, 1989.
- *One of the best overviews of the benchmarking process.*

Chase, Richard B., and Robert H. Hayes. "Beefing Up Operations in Service Firms." *Sloan Management Review*, 33 (Fall 1991), pp. 15-26.
- *Examines how value is added in service operations and elaborates on the attributes of various stages of development for service organizations.*

Ettorre, Barbara, "Benchmarking: The Next Generation." *Management Review* (June 1993), pp. 42-62.
- *This article provides a solid insight into where benchmarking may be going. It also gives specific information on various benchmarking organizations.*

Fink, Ronald. "America's Most Imitated Companies." *Financial World* 162 (Sept. 28, 1993), pp. 42-62.
- *Provides considerable information on the practice of benchmarking. It offers detailed scenarios of how 11 companies use benchmarking in specific areas.*

Ford, Donald J., "Benchmarking HRD." *Training and Development*, June 1993, pp. 36-41.
- *Offers a good example of how benchmarking is now moving into internal service unit specialties.*

Fuller, F. Timothy, "Eliminating Complexity from Work: Improving Productivity by Enhancing Quality." *National Productivity Review*, Autumn, 1985, pp. 327-344.
- *Offers an interesting look at how Hewlett-Packard analyzed and attacked complexity.*

Hall, Gene, Jim Rosenthal, and Judy Wade. "How to Make Reengineering Really Work." *Harvard Business Review* (November/December 1993), pp. 119-131.
- *Challenges some of the success claims of the reengineering movement.*

Hammer, Michael and James Champy. *Reengineering the Corporation: A Manifesto for Business Revolution.* New York, NY, HarperBusiness, 1993.
- *Calls for a total re-examination of the basic premises of what is done and why it is done throughout business. The suggested approach is to throw away the existing blueprint and begin anew to identify those things that are absolutely essential to the fundamental tasks.*

Hart, Christopher, "The Power of Internal Guarantees." *Harvard Business Review*, January/February 1995, pp. 64-73.
- *Examines the payoffs for external customers of internal service commitments*

Hufnagel, Ellen M., and Jacob G. Birnberg. "Perceived Chargeback Fairness in Decentralized Organizations: An Examination of the Issues." *MIS Quarterly*, 13, (December 1989), pp. 415-430.
- *Addresses concerns about fairness in internal chargeback systems. In particular, it examines how fairness perceptions are influenced by: 1) a high degree of interdependence, 2) restrictions on alternative purchase alternatives, and 3) the tendency for full cost to exceed market prices.*

Leth, Steven A. "The Five Best Practices of Service Leadership." *National Productivity Review*, 9, no. 2, (Spring 1990), pp. 201-212.
- *Reports on the specific service practices in place in 40 service firms.*

PART VI: IMPLEMENTATION

Adler, Paul S., "Time-and-Motion Regained." *Harvard Business Review,* January/February, 1993, pp. 97-108.
- *Offers a recount of the dramatic changes at the NUMMI plant in California.*

Barker, Joel, "Discovering the Future: The Business of Paradigms," Charthouse International, Burnsville, MN, (800) 328-3789.
- *This videotape challenges the basic paradigms of an organization.*

Bowen, David E. and Edward E. Lawler III. "The Empowerment of Service Workers: What, Why, How, and When." *Sloan Management Review* (Spring 1992), pp. 48-60.
- *Does an excellent job of challenging the premise that all empowerment is good. It takes a reasoned approach to examination of the specific variables and situations that may make empowerment appropriate.*

Deal, Terrence E., and Allan A. Kennedy. *Corporate Cultures: The Rites and Rituals of Corporate Life,* Addison-Wesley, Reading, MA, 1982.
- *Explores the workings of a corporate culture.*

Frey, Robert. "Empowerment or Else." *Harvard Business Review* (September/October 1993), pp. 80-94.
- *First-person story relates how one CEO concluded that moving authority to his employees was his only viable option and the route that he took to execute it.*

Garvin, David A. "Building a Learning Organization." *Harvard Business Review* (July/August 1993), pp. 78-91.
- *Examines the nature of a learning organization and shows why this characteristic is so vital to success.*

Gross, Tracy, Richard Pascale, and Anthony Athos. "The Reinvention Roller Coaster: Risking the Present for a Powerful Future." *Harvard Business Review*, (November/December 1993), pp. 97-108.
- *Expresses the pressing need to do much more than just incremental change in most organizations is explored in this article that has particular relevance for internal service organizations contemplating massive change.*

Kotter, John P., and James L. Heskett. *Corporate Culture and Performance*, Free Press, New York, NY, 1992.
- *Provides a critical analysis of the powerful relationship between an organization's culture and its performance.*

Scholtes, Peter R., *The Team Handbook: How to Use Teams to Improve Quality*, Joiner Associates, Madison, WI, pp. 1988.
- *A practical handbook for use by implementation teams in the quality process.*

Senge, Peter M., *The Fifth Discipline: The Art & Practice of the Learning Organization*, Doubleday, New York, NY, 1990.
- *Provides an in-depth look at organizational "learning disabilities" that tend to limit progress and inhibit growth. Senge outlines five disciplines that allow organizations to overcome these difficulties.*

Senge, Peter M., et. al., *The Fifth Discipline Fieldbook: Strategies and Tools for Building a Learning Organization*, Currency Doubleday, New York, NY, 1994.
- *Assembles an eclectic catalogue of work from various writers that applies the concepts in the original book and establishes a continuing dialogue on organizational learning.*

Teal, Thomas. "Service Comes First: An Interview with USAA's Robert F. McDermott." *Harvard Business Review* (September-October 1991), pp. 117-127.
- *Shows how the United Services Automobile Association (USAA) is an insurer that has built an extremely strong reputation as a service-centered company. In this interview, the CEO of USAA describes how "culture" is the key factor that makes USAA the effective company that it is today.*

INDEX
— A —

— B —

— C —

— D —

— E —

— F —

facilities, 15, 16, 19
Federal Express Corp., 35, 126, 127, 128, 136, 203
Federal Reserve, 137
final commitment, 75, 82–85
finance *See* accounting/finance
First Commerce Corp., New Orleans, 83, 174
"fishbone diagram", 106
flawed contribution, 17
forcesat work, 37–66, 206; emerging,
    downward spiral,59–66
Ford, Henry, 155
Ford Motor Co., 48
Four Seasons Hotel, 165
franchisor, 101

— G —

Gallup survey, 161
General Electric, 137
General Motors, 168, 169
"gotcha!", 63, 64
Granier, James, C., 83
Greyson, Jonathan; fictitious name *See* Mid-Americorp
GTE, 120, 134, 202
guarantees of internal performance, 133, 134

— H —

Hackett Group (Cleveland, Oh.), 136
Hammer, Michael, 120
Hampden-Turner, Charles, 160
Hanson Industries Limited, 25
hardware, 70
Hay Group, 53
Hazen, Paul, 54, 55
headquarters, 15, 16, 22, 25
heroes and culture, 155, 156
Heskett, James, Harvard Business School, 153, 183, 184
Hirschhorn, Larry, 48
historical improvement attention, 16
historical performance attention, xi
historical security, 46
historical service, 99, 114
human resources, 15–17, 19, 27, 38, 51, 134, 136, 155, 158
human-centered approaches, 52, 104, 158

— I —

IBM Corp., 22, 52, 152, 153, 201
implementation, 68, 88, 110, 141–181, 210– 211
increasing internal service productivity, 34
industrial companies, 53
inefficient service, 28, 45, 54, 55, 138
information; customer unit as source of, 102–105
information architecture, 52
information gathering, 68, 88–94, 110, 142, 161
information and introspection, 95–110
information systems, 15, 17, 19, 27, 31, 38,
 52, 53, 59, 62, 104, 137, 158; bank case
 study *See* Mid-Americorp
integration, quest, 121
internal performance, guarantees of, 133, 134
internal service crisis, 13–35, 205–206
internal service degenerative scenario, 62
internal service development stages, 119
internal service renaissance option, 32, 33
internal service selected readings, 205–211
internal service symptoms of serious problems, 27
International Benchmarking Clearinghouse, 136
interview outline for key customer
 representatives, 195–197
introspection and information, 95–110
Intuit, Quicken software, 99
ISU, internal service unit defined, 27

— J —

Jobs, Steven, 152, 155

— K —

Kearney, A. T., 136
Kodak, 46
Kotter, John, Harvard Business School, 153, 184

— L —

language and culture, 154
Lawler III, Edward, 167
Lawrence, Paul, 121
Layton, Rear Admiral Edwin T., 33
Lee, Chris, 61
legal services, 15, 16, 19, 51
line units, 15, 18, 62, 132

— P —

— Q —

— R —

recruitment, 17
Renaissance, 32–35, 38, 64, 73, 104, 107
research and development, 15–17, 19, 49, 52, 101, 121
research function, customer, 35
resistance, anticipate, 178
resources, control of, 18
responsibility, segmentation of ownership, 100
reward systems and culture, 157, 159
Rinehart, Jim, 48
Rockefeller, John D., 155
Rogers, Carl, 173
role of culture, 151–154
role of ISUs, 15–21, 96, 100–102
roles, supervisory, 166–168
Roosevelt, President, 156
Rosie the Riveter, 156

— S —

safety vs. macho, 160
sales, 19, 21, 38
Saratoga Institute, (Saratoga, Calif.), 136
Scandinavian Airlines System (SAS), 103
scatter diagram, work process analysis tools, 105, 106
scenario of degenerative internal service, 62
Schiemenn & Associates, 19
Scholtes, Peter, 106
self-study, conducting, 95–110
self-study action steps, 90, 91
service; complexity, 55–57
service; culture vs. professionalism, 157, 158
service; duplication, 41, 60
service; inefficient ,28, 45, 54, 55
service; outsourcing, 32, 46, 70
service people, development of, 161–171
service problem identification and recovery, 126, 135
service quality index (SQI), 126
service standards, building, 112–114, 121, 122
service strategy, 117–129
service and support costs; percent of, 21
service unit; how it sees itself, 96–98
service unit perspective, 63
service unit roles, 100, 101
service-profit chain, 17
situational assessment, 75–79
six-sigma quality program, 127
Smith, Fred, 126
Snow, Dennis A., 155
software, 56, 70, 99
Square D Co., 98, 99